For Gabbie
Happy 30th ♡

THE FATE OF THE LAND
LIES NOT IN THE HANDS
OF ITS OWNERS
FALSE AND TRUE
BUT NATURE WILL THRIVE
WHEN THE COMMONS ARISE
IN THE FACTIONS
OF WE FIND OUR HOME

THE
TRESPASSER'S
COMPANION

**A field guide to reclaiming
what is already ours**

NICK HAYES

BLOOMSBURY PUBLISHING
LONDON · OXFORD · NEW YORK · NEW DELHI · SYDNEY

BLOOMSBURY PUBLISHING
Bloomsbury Publishing Plc
50 Bedford Square, London, WC1B 3DP, UK
29 Earlsfort Terrace, Dublin 2, Ireland

BLOOMSBURY, BLOOMSBURY PUBLISHING and the Diana logo are
trademarks of Bloomsbury Publishing Plc

First published in Great Britain 2022

A catalogue record for this book is available from the British Library

ISBN: HB: 978-1-5266-4645-3; eBook: 978-1-5266-4644-6; ePDF: 978-1-
5266-4646-0

2 4 6 8 10 9 7 5 3 1

Designed by Nick Hayes and Clare Baggaley
Printed and bound in Great Britain by CPI Group (UK) Ltd, Croydon
CR0 4YY

**To find out more about our authors and books visit
www.bloomsbury.com and sign up for our newsletters**

"THE PRINCIPLE
OF DIRECT ACTION
IS THE DEFIANT
INSISTENCE
ON ACTING AS IF
ONE IS ALREADY FREE"

DAVID GRAEBER

CONTENTS

FOREWORD

Charles Darwin, England's most treasured naturalist, grew up in his parents' home, a manor house with a seven-acre estate near Shrewsbury in Shropshire. He was raised with the right to roam through a broad expanse of nature, and by crawling on his hands and knees through woodland, by upturning stones and fallen logs, he discovered not just earwigs and worms but a love of discovery itself. Close observation, exploration, fascination, wonder – the whole course of science changed not in the *Beagle*'s voyage to the Galapagos but in those seven acres in the West Midlands.

But Darwin came from great wealth. His father was a society doctor and financier and his mother was a millionaire in her own right. His seven acres, which he later described as a 'paradise', was a walled garden, and luckily for Darwin – and for science – he was born inside those walls. Yet today, one in eight families in the UK (3.3 million people) have no access to a garden, let alone an estate several acres wide. In fact, while half of England belongs to just 1 per cent of us, 55 million citizens own an average of 0.07 acres. Without broader rights to explore nature, how many children are denied the right to hold snails, to find frogs, to catalogue beetles, and in turn, how many geniuses is English culture denied?

PREVIOUS PAGE *Charles Darwin*   ABOVE *Darwin's childhood garden*

We have the right to adventure through just 8 per cent of England, those remote areas of open access that fall under the Countryside and Rights of Way (CRoW) Act of 2000. We are legally allowed to explore a mere 3 per cent of our rivers. Granted, we have 144,000 miles of footpath to walk in England and Wales, yet this accounts for just 0.3 per cent of the landmass. Besides, following a footpath hardly counts as adventure: off these paths, there is so much more to see. And so much more to do.

On Saturday 24 April 2021, Extinction Rebellion and Right to Roam organised a mass trespass of local areas across the country. Up to a hundred groups – families, friends, individuals – went out along the paths they had come to know so well during lockdown. But this time they overstepped the boundaries that kept them out of nature. They explored, many for the first time, the woods and the meadows, the lakes and the rivers of their home. One particular trespass stood out. A professional botanist climbed the fence of a patch of ground five minutes from his house. While wandering through forbidden ground, he found a sub-species of dandelion, *Taraxacum subhamatum*, previously unrecorded in East Anglia. Twelve years he'd lived there, obeying the limits to his curiosity, wonder and expertise, and for twelve years East Anglia was barred from a fuller knowledge of itself. How much greater would our understanding be of the nature of England, not to mention the nature of Englishness, if we were granted access to it?

Why have we come to accept the limitations on our wonder? How have we become acclimatised to the militarisation of our countryside, the miles of barbed wire that exclude us from our meadows, the razor fences that drive us away from our rivers with the explicit threat of violence? When exactly did it become acceptable that our appreciation of the diversity of nature be confined to paths alone? Without a truly experiential, immersed connection to nature, how are we supposed to care about it and – just as crucially – care for it?

We can get angry, or we can get organised – we who believe that a greater connection to nature improves our mental and physical health, who recognise that some communities are more marginalised than others, who believe that a greater immersion in nature is the cure not only for our ills but also for those of nature itself. Individually, we can break the rules as often as we like, but as with every right that has been won in history, only together can we change them.

This book is the little sister of *The Book of Trespass*. While that book set out the context, the historical progression and the ongoing social injustice of our exclusion from the English countryside, this book is a plan (and a provocation) to change the definition of how we connect to nature – from a crime, to a birthright. It is not an incitement to break the law, it is a call to change it. Treat its chapters like ingredients in a spell, a spell that when enacted together, en masse, can turn one step over the line into a dissolution of the line itself.

This is not a book to sit on your shelf; it will start to howl if you leave it indoors for too long. It wants mud on its spine, leaf litter in its binding, and feathers between its pages. Take it out with you, do some of the things it suggests, find others who are reading the book, go out with them. Because the heart and soul of this book is action. In the words of Dame Freya Stark, one of England's greatest explorers, 'There can be no happiness if the things we believe in are different from the things we do.' So we trespass.

'If we have more opportunities to spend time in restorative natural environments, then we will be happier and healthier – the science is unequivocal on that.'

LUCY JONES, AUTHOR OF
*LOSING EDEN: WHY OUR
MINDS NEED THE WILD*

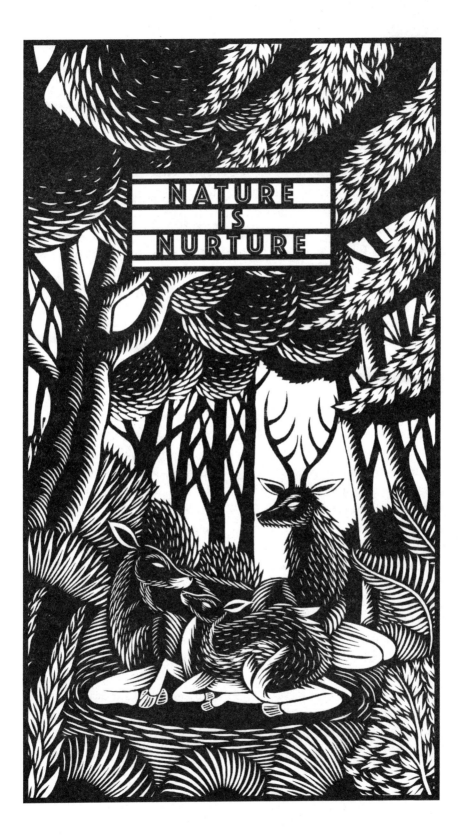

Throughout human history, medics, poets, shamans and philosophers across the globe have underlined the vital link between nature and human health. Without it, we wither; with it, we flourish. But only recently has science begun to prove with empirical evidence what we, in ourselves, have known all along: in body, mind and soul, nature heals us.

The desire to access our countryside, to experience its nature, has for too long been polarised into partisan politics, the Left trying to get one over on the Right and the Right doubling down to save face. But this matter is too important for wearying tribalism. It's time to change the conversation: public access is a matter of public health. For all of us, nature is nurture.

Body

Nature not only provides us the necessary open space to exercise – to swim, climb, cycle, paddle, walk and run – but also offers a whole host of benefits for our body while we do so. From the microbes in the ground, which stimulate our brain to release serotonin, to the gentle sounds of birdsong or flowing water, the gentle green-and-blue chaos of nature gives us a holistic sense of well-being that compliments exercise, an added gift from nature that makes its health benefits much greater than exercising in a gym or an urban environment.

Walking up hill and down dale is fantastic aerobic exercise, as good for the arteries as it is for the thighs, and has been shown to reduce cardiovascular and pulmonary heart disease. Regular exercise helps reduce obesity, and as a result reduces the effects of diabetes and hypertension. This is nature as a gymnasium, but it also offers pharmaceutical benefits. The Japanese practice of *shinrin-yoku*, or forest bathing, is becoming increasingly popular, with the science behind it as solid as its cultural legacy. If you're walking, jogging, meditating or simply relaxing among the trees, you are breathing in the essential oils they produce, which has a fortifying effect on your immune system. Just a two-hour dip in the forest air can strengthen your immune system for up to thirty days afterwards.

Similarly, while swimming is great exercise, swimming in the cold water of lakes, reservoirs or rivers

simply multiplies its beneficial effects. On its simplest level, it helps us burn fat: by exercising in cold water, we burn more calories than in a swimming pool. It goes further. Regular cold immersion controls the concentration of uric acid in our blood, which reduces swelling, easing the pain of arthritis and speeding up recovery and rehabilitation after surgery.

Cold-water swimming has even been shown to ease the effects of menopause. Though English society does its best to ignore it, menopause affects half of our population, and the symptoms can be so strong that they have a significant effect on women's everyday activities. The most common symptom is the hot flush, and the impact of cold water on the body has been shown to boost circulation, speed up metabolism and maintain a stable core temperature, all of which can help regulate the

frequency and intensity of hot flushes. Many women find it hard to sleep when transitioning through the menopause, and 61 per cent of postmenopausal women experience frequent bouts of insomnia. But cold-water immersion stimulates the body's parasympathetic nervous system, which is responsible for repairing the body, and promotes a general feeling of calm and contentment. Cold water also eases the pain of joint inflammation, and even helps to combat the decrease in libido associated with menopause. A NASA study in 2012, which mapped responses over twelve weeks, discovered that the body adapts to the cold over time, a process that reduces cholesterol, inhibits blood clotting and increases both fertility and libido.

Mind

Nature can make us feel better about ourselves. It can alleviate the effects of stress, depression, anxiety, post-traumatic stress disorder (PTSD) and attention deficit hyperactivity disorder (ADHD). As American journalist Florence Williams writes in *Nature Fix: Why Nature Makes Us Happier, Healthier and More Creative*: 'When we spend time outside in beautiful places, a part of our brain called the subgenual prefrontal cortex quiets down, and this is the part of the brain that

is associated with negative self-reported rumination.' A study in Stanford, California found that a fifty-minute walk in nature, as compared with the busy streets of Palo Alto, resulted in both 'affective benefits' (decreased anxiety, rumination and negative affect, and the preservation of positive affect) and 'cognitive benefits' (increased working-memory performance). The scientists from the study suggested the following explanation: 'Nature experience may decrease rumination in participants due to an increased focus on aspects of the environment that are not directly related to narratives about the self.' In other words, it is helpful to humans to observe the myriad events of a non-human world, to draw us out of our anthropocentric mindsets.

Simply breathing in the fresh air of open spaces can encourage our brains to grow. *Neuroplasticity* is the term given to the brain's ability to form and reorganise synaptic connections, which can help with learning, but also, in terms of depression and anxiety, help to organise our thoughts more constructively. Nature encourages our brain to find different routes, making more positive connections.

The mental benefits of cold-water immersion come not just from the cold itself, but from the sheer shock it exerts on us. The body does not differentiate between the whys and wherefores of stress, and regardless of whether it is a pile of unpaid bills, a divorce or a hectic day at work, the body reacts to each situation in the same way – fight or flight, releasing cortisol into the blood and increasing the heart rate. By immersing ourselves regularly in cold water, we effectively train our body to remain calm in stressful situations, not only helping us to survive if we happen to fall into a body of water, but also to remain composed and focused in life's melee of stress-inducing scenarios. Similar effects can be achieved in the shower – except, of course, wagtails don't visit you at home in the bathroom.

In his 1973 book *The Anatomy of Human Destructiveness*, the psychoanalyst Erich Fromm coined the term 'biophilia' to describe 'the passionate love of life and of all that is alive'. Ten years later, the concept of biophilia was adopted by Edward O. Wilson in his book of the same name, which proposed that our innate human affiliation with nature and non-human life forms has, in part, a genetic basis. This theory has been developed through research, and it has recently been proposed that our immune system depends on certain microbes that evolved in unison with the human organism. As a result, their absence in our lives is thought to cause abnormal functionality of the immune system and an increased susceptibility not just to allergies but also sensations of anxiety. This theory looks at the other side of the coin: how being deprived of nature estranges us from elements that our bodies have evolved to rely on.

Soul

Nature is the original mosque, synagogue, church and temple. The bowers of great trees gave us shade and shelter in which to congregate, and the many minor miracles of its flora and fauna, not to mention its vast vistas, gave us our original contact with the *numinous* – that feeling of something much greater at play than the intricacies of our life. There is something Great out there.

Since the Romans introduced it to England, the term 'pagan' has always been used in a derogatory sense. The original meaning of the Latin *paganus* was simply 'rustic', but like the modern 'yokel' or 'hick',

it came to mean uncivilised, crude and, in the Roman army, bad at soldiering. By the Middle Ages, it had come to refer to any religion outside of Christianity, specifically polytheistic, animist religions that worshipped natural entities over man-made gods.

After many hundreds of years of negative conditioning, it is understandable that people don't like to identify as pagan. But drop the word, unshackle the label, and you're still left with the unnegotiable fact that when sunk in nature, everything around you is alive. And simply in terms of the life-giving properties of trees and rivers, the way they generate life and sustain it, they do seem to fit the job description of gods.

Nature's effect on us is not confined to our bodies and minds, but can improve more abstract elements in us. Nature can make us kinder, or in scientific terms, it has been shown to improve our 'prosociality'. In one study by the

University of California, Berkeley, scientists found that being exposed to nature improved our prosocial tendencies, as measured by agreeableness, perspective-taking and empathy. The researchers found that nature can make us more generous and trusting and that, when surrounded by plants, we become more helpful to each other.

Nature can make us happier, and it can make us more creative. A study published in the *Journal of Environmental Psychology* (2014) found that walking in nature in urban environments decreased the levels of salivary cortisol, a key biological indicator for heightened stress levels. In the words of the University of Utah's David Strayer: 'If you've been using your brain to multitask – as most of us do most of the day – and then you set that aside and go on a walk, without all of the gadgets, you've let the prefrontal cortex recover. And that's when we see these bursts in creativity, problem solving and feelings of well-being.'

But nature can also console us, bring us together and unite us, and this is vital for addressing England's most unacknowledged public health crisis. Loneliness is an epidemic of entirely different dimensions to obesity or Covid-19.

Loneliness has a catastrophic impact on mental health, on community cohesion, on the National Health Service and on our economy, but there is a stigma attached to it, and for this reason it is rarely spoken of. According to research carried out in 2016, over 9 million UK adults – almost a fifth of the population – feel lonely all or most of the time. For 41 per cent of people in the UK aged over sixty-five, a pet or TV is their main source of company. And yet loneliness is more common among our young people than our old. According to the BBC's recent 'Loneliness Experiment', 40 per cent of young people reported feeling lonely 'often' or 'very often', compared with 27 per cent of those over seventy-five.

The UK government's recent 25 Year Environment Plan makes it clear that nature can help: 'Spending time in the natural environment – as a resident or a visitor – improves our mental health ... It can combat loneliness and bind communities together.' There is something in nature that allows the loneliest, shyest and most anxious people of our communities to feel a part of life without having to abide by the etiquettes and expectations of society. Solitude can be a whole lot more wholesome than loneliness, and nature does solitude like nothing else.

Another aspect to connecting with nature is the camaraderie and social connections it encourages. Cold-water swimming groups are as much about the collective overcoming of the barrier of coldness as they are about the health benefits you receive from doing so. Meeting in the morning before work and dunking yourself in a frozen lake bonds you with the people you do it with.

Nature encourages group participation: walking and swimming, certainly, but also drawing, writing and exploration – activities that can be done alone or in groups. The Wildlife Trusts is an organisation that runs hundreds of local volunteering groups across the country, bringing people together to get outside, protect nature, exercise and socialise. Last year, they engaged half a million people in their events and activities, which incorporated group walks and volunteering in wildlife sanctuaries. An independent study by the University of Essex into Wildlife Trusts volunteering programmes found that 95 per cent of participants with low well-being who volunteered outdoors once a week reported an improvement in their mental health in just six weeks. By engaging with nature, we are engaging with each other; by helping nature, we are actually helping ourselves.

Lucy Jones
Author of Losing Eden:
Why Our Minds Need the Wild

In my twenties, while living in London, working as a journalist, I had a pretty standard-level disconnection from the natural world. My life from a teenager into adulthood was all about pubs, clubs, gigs and work, and at twenty-seven I finally admitted that my relationship with alcohol and other substances had become unmanageable, and I needed to find other ways to alleviate the episodes of depression and general anxiety I was experiencing.

I quit drinking, went into recovery, attended support groups and saw psychiatrists and psychotherapists, but I was still looking for something that could somehow steady the raw emotions of sobriety. I needed to soothe the psychological storm and clear my head, so I tried running. But, more often than not, I would get distracted, slow down and end up looking at trees and kestrels, insects and flowers. I'd get lost for a couple of hours on Walthamstow Marshes. And then, when back in my flat, I felt like a completely different person: the angry, critical voices in my head were quietened; my brain was scoured clean and restored.

At the time, it wasn't obvious to me that nature could help my mental health. It wasn't suggested to me – not by medics or by my friends – because, culturally speaking, there wasn't the same mainstream dialogue about nature and mental health as there is today. But there it was, really helping me. I wanted to investigate, to find out how this powerful effect could come about, what was really happening to my body, brain and mind, and that's what led to my book.

If we have more opportunities to spend time in restorative natural environments, then we will be happier and healthier – the science is unequivocal on that. But as I got deeper into the research, the question switched in my head from how nature helps our minds, to how our estrangement from the living world harms us. It became evident that time apart from nature is leeching our mental health, that almost everyone is under the healthy baseline. Current theories – the 'Prospect Refuge' theory, biophilia, the 'Old Friends' theory – suggest we evolved alongside our environment, that the microorganisms that live in our gut need the chemicals of the natural world to function properly. There's a reason that petrichor (the aroma of the earth after it's rained) smells so good to us – we have evolved to be attuned to irrigated landscapes, where water could be easily found.

I love the idea that we humans are porous to the natural world, that we're not adamantine, but that our insides interact with the outside world. What we do to the world, we do to ourselves. It happens for the worse, with studies now showing a link between air pollution and psychotic experiences and schizophrenia, or when chemicals in exhaust fumes have been shown to cross over from mother to baby through the placenta. But it also works for the better, with bacteria found in soil (such as *Mycobacterium vaccae*) having an antidepressant-like effect on the brain, activating neurons that produce serotonin, which may explain why gardeners get a buzz from growing. But it feels like we have only scratched the surface of how microbacteria react with our bodies, and this is an area that needs a lot more study.

I think we need to change the way we talk about the living world. 'Green space', 'biodiversity', even the word 'nature' are beginning to sound like terms from a textbook, and don't acknowledge the wonder and awe and thrill we feel within it, the strong emotional impact it has on us. If we want to orient people towards natural spaces, to fight for natural spaces to be protected, we need to rediscover a kinship and communion with the living world. To stop trashing the planet in the way that we are doing, we need to collectively fall back in love with the rest of nature – and our language needs to express that. The issue is that we see ourselves as separate: what we call 'the environment', we should instead call our home.

THE NATURAL HEALTH SERVICE

After the Second World War, Clement Attlee's government began designing a new architecture for the state, a welfare system for the people of Britain that protected them from poverty and ill health. Alongside state pensions, unemployment income and the National Health Service, a full right to roam was considered across the British Isles.

Giving people access rights to swim and walk in the countryside they had fought for was presented as a vital support system for the new NHS. When so many conditions, mental and physical, can be mitigated or alleviated by access to nature, it seemed clear that opening up more land to public access would benefit the public. In this way, what is sometimes called the 'Natural

Health Service' would nurture people's well-being, while the National Health Service could focus more on medical intervention. Nature would work hand-in-hand with nurses, taking a holistic approach to our nation's health.

Solicitor and Liberal politician Sir Arthur Hobhouse was commissioned to investigate, and his report, published in 1947, recommended expanding access to the countryside. Two years later, many of its suggestions were written into a bill for parliament, which became the National Parks Act of 1949. The bill proposed the creation of a series of national parks, twelve in all, that would be designated spaces of nature conservation and public access. It demanded a map of the networks of rights of way (which, incidentally, is still being compiled to this day) and the provision of penalties for landowners who blocked them or erected signage discouraging people from using them.

On the second reading, this radical approach to public access was still embedded within the bill, and excitement was building over what would be 'an effective contribution … to the health and well-being of the nation, and an important step taken towards establishing the principle that the heritage of our beautiful countryside should be held in trust for the benefit of the people'. Lewis Silkin, then minister of town and country planning, continued:

> **This is not just a bill. It is a people's charter – a people's charter for the open air, for the hikers and the ramblers, for everyone who lives to get out into the open air and enjoy the countryside. Without it they are fettered, deprived of their powers of access and facilities needed to make holidays enjoyable. With it the countryside is theirs to preserve, to cherish, to enjoy and to make their own.**

However, somewhere between the second reading and the passing of the bill – in other words, when it got to the major landowners of the House of Lords – the 'access' part of the bill was muted, buried and forgotten. The actual title of the act was the National Parks and Access to the Countryside Act, but because the provisions for public access have been so watered down, people today forget the last half of its title. And while it did provide a structure for landowners to dedicate their land to public access, if they so wished, the radical change in our relationship to the countryside all but disappeared. To introduce an English right to roam now would simply be to complete the initial vision that led to the institution of our national parks and to reinstate a vital support network for our nation's most treasured institution, the NHS.

During the pandemic, the mantra from the government came loud and clear: we had to alleviate the pressure on the NHS. But the truth is, the NHS has been operating beyond its capacity since its creation, and as early as 1949 it began charging for prescriptions and rolling back the services it offered, such as free glasses and false teeth. The answer to this problem has always been to privatise either some or all of the services, but there is another way.

The overall cost to the economy of physical inactivity in England is estimated by NHS Forest (a project coordinated by the Centre for Sustainable Healthcare) to be £8.2 billion per year. As a result, the value of encouraging people to be active is huge, with NHS Forest reporting that simply 'reducing the sedentary population by one percent could reduce both morbidity and mortality rates at £1.44 billion a year'. The financial impact of mental illness on people's quality of life is even more alarming, with the National Mental Health Development Unit estimating losses of £41.8 billion per year in England, while the related costs to the national economy of welfare payments and lost productivity are thought to be somewhere in the region of £77 billion per year.

Only very recently, England has caught on to New Zealand's long-practised technique of 'green prescriptions'. In July 2020, the UK environment secretary, George Eustice, announced a £4 million investment project aimed at preventing and tackling mental ill health through 'green social prescribing'. Green prescriptions are simply advice to go out and ease the condition through regular physical activity and nutritional adjustments. In New Zealand, a country that has been doling out green prescriptions for decades, they have been shown to improve mental health outcomes, reduce health inequalities, reduce demand on the health and social care system and make outdoor activities more accessible. Research from NHS Forest states that six to eight months after receiving their green prescription, 63 per cent of patients are more active than they were before and 46 per cent have lost weight.

The elephant in the room, of course, is that we are still actively discouraged from entering the countryside. Open access to just 8 per cent of our land and 3 per cent of rivers limits our ability to incorporate exercise into our lives. However, this paucity of access builds a deeper trench between the public and nature by creating a general sense of unwelcomeness – a sense that we are not invited into our beautiful English countryside, that we are in fact breaking some legal and moral code by being there at all. So, for many, the idea of taking a dip in a river is not just prevented by the law, it is forgotten about entirely.

Imagine going into a pharmacy and having access to only 3 per cent of its shelves, or going into a gym to find that 92 per cent of the equipment is behind barbed wire. It wouldn't be long before you stopped bothering with the gym and pharmacy altogether. Until we tackle the stark inadequacy of our access to nature, any state-led attempts to improve our nation's health will be applying a Band-Aid to a broken leg. The government can produce as many pamphlets and run as many marketing schemes as it likes, but until the countryside is opened up, the culture of England will remain sedentary, and the health of the nation will continue to suffer.

'When you're forced to stick to
the roads or the pathways, your
experience of nature is very passive;
it privileges the visual sense over
all others. You become an observer
of nature, not a part of it. To
experience nature, to feel that sense
of belonging, I have to trespass.'

JON MOSES,
DOCTOR OF PHENOMENOLOGY

Trespass falls under a section of law called tort, a word whose origins are from the French, meaning 'damage'. Tort is like that drawer in your house where you put everything that doesn't have an obvious home elsewhere. It is a miscellany of misdemeanour, comprising libel, slander, nuisance, negligence, assault and battery, defamation, detinue and conversion, and cases can include anything from a dog bite to a false allegation in the press. Tort law covers anything that constitutes damage to someone, be it their reputation or personhood or property, which are all considered to be one and the same thing. And there, right at the top of the drawer, like a banana in a toolkit, is trespass.

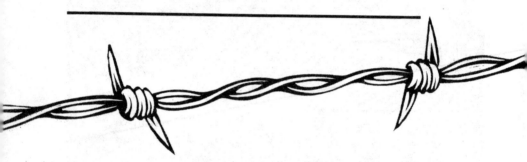

The whole architecture of trespass law rests upon the shaky construct that, by simply being on land you don't own, you are causing damage not just to the land but also to the owner. Actual harm done to property is covered by the law of criminal damage, and yet since a precedent was set in the nineteenth century, the public have been compelled to accept that swimming in a river or walking in woodland is harmful to its owner. This construct is known in law as a 'legal fiction', a leap of logic built into the legal system that merely serves the system and not the people. Simply put, a legal fiction is 'an assertion that is accepted as true for legal purposes, even though it may be untrue or unproven'. And, what do you know, the example given by the Oxford Dictionary to illustrate the definition is as follows: 'One must remember that landownership is ultimately simply a legal fiction.'

The legal fiction that trespass is harmful to the landowner has become so internalised within the English psyche that we accept it over and above the evidence of our own eyes and bodies. The idea of trespass as harm has also been extrapolated to the unprovable bias that any trespass is also harmful to the ecology. Acolytes of this legal fiction are very vocal in expressing the idea that even though no harm has occurred during a trespass, harm has occurred *by* the trespass. Yet the law itself accepts this as fiction, and simply uses it as a way of polyfilling up the holes in its own architecture. If there is harm in trespass, it is not to the landowner or the land, but to the general public, who are denied the many benefits of nature simply to sustain the lunacy of the law.

THE LAWS OF TRESPASS

Trespass

There are three main types of trespass: trespass *to the person*, trespass *to goods* and trespass *to land*, which applies equally to water and air. Trespass to the person consists of three varieties: (1) assault, which is 'to act in such a way that the claimant believes he is about to be attacked'; (2) battery, which is 'the intentional and direct application of force to another person'; and (3) false imprisonment, which is 'depriving the claimant of freedom of movement, without a lawful justification for doing so'. All three of these are based on the principle that 'any person's body is inviolate'.

Trespass to goods is defined simply as 'wrongful physical interference with goods that are in the possession of another'. This 'interference' can consist of anything between touching and moving, and applies regardless of intent or damage. For all those with a habit of leaving their wet towels on the bedroom floor, only to be tidied up by another, it is worth remembering that the former can potentially sue the latter for trespass to goods.

Trespass to land involves the 'unjustifiable interference with land which is in the immediate and exclusive possession of another'; it is both a tort and, in certain circumstances, a crime under

the Criminal Justice and Public Order Act of 1994. Trespass to land is actionable *per se*. In other words, it does not need evidence of actual damage to be considered harmful; it is a harm in and of itself. Not meaning to trespass, or not knowing you're trespassing, is of no consequence to the law and is still actionable.

Trespass refers not just to when you intrude on land that you don't own, but also when you happen to be on someone's property and your permission to be there expires. If you're walking on National Trust parkland past closing time, you are trespassing. If you're in a cinema and misbehave to the point where the owner asks you to leave, you have invalidated your right to be on the premises and therefore you are trespassing.

PUNISHMENT:

Nothing. You'll be asked to leave, and if you do so, that's the sum of it. If the police are called and you resist them, you can be arrested for a breach of the peace.

Aggravated Trespass

Aggravated trespass applies in circumstances where you, and at least one other person, are trespassing 'with intent'. It was a law invented for the Criminal Justice and Public Order Act 1994 for the purpose of clearing hunt saboteurs, travellers and ravers, but it applies equally to picnickers and amateur entomologists. The prosecution must prove not that any intimidation of the landowner occurred, but simply that this was the intent. Use of insulting language will support their allegation of intimidation. The order to leave can only be made by a senior police officer present at the scene, and they must reasonably believe the following: that there are two or more trespassers, they have a common purpose of residing on the land, the occupier has taken reasonable steps to ask them to leave, and the trespassers have either caused damage to the land or property on it or have used insulting words or behaviour to the occupier.

PUNISHMENT:

Maximum penalty is three months' imprisonment, or a fine of £2,500, or both. First-time offenders can expect a fine of £200–£300.

Criminal Trespass

For the last couple of decades, trespass has been considered a criminal act on sixteen selected sites across the UK. Under the broad title of 'Terrorism and Organised Crime', Sections 128–131 of the Serious Organised Crime and Police Act 2005 expressly forbid entry to certain sites, punishable with up to a year in prison. This act applies, very reasonably, to sites of national security, such as the Ministry of Defence in Whitehall or Government Communications Headquarters (GCHQ) sites, and likewise to all licensed nuclear sites, but also to the hundreds of acres of private and Crown land belonging to the Queen. This includes the Home Park, a 400-acre royal park which borders the Thames in Berkshire and which used to be a public park up until 1847.

But 2021 brought a new, conveniently vague expansion to the criminalisation of trespass. For over a decade now, certain factions of the government have been lobbying for laws to criminalise the way of life of the travelling community. The 2019 Conservative manifesto included a pledge to criminalise trespass

with intent to reside – criminalising not the travel but its inevitable consequence, the brief and temporary stopping on land. The new Police, Crime, Sentencing and Courts Bill fulfils this promise, and the Conservatives have successfully landed another blow to an already marginalised community. The proposal has changed a little since it was first mooted. From its inception, the criminalisation of trespass was seen as a direct blow to the travelling community, attracting attention from human rights groups. The police themselves repeatedly said they didn't want these new powers, and that a greater provision of temporary stopping sites would be a much more feasible solution. So, to slip through the net of human rights lawyers, the Conservatives have broadened the definition of criminal trespass to include anyone who turns up on land they don't own, in possession of a vehicle with the intent to reside. The Conservatives have blurred and broadened the category to incorporate many more communities: van dwellers, mountain bikers, kayakers and wild campers.

And yet the rotten core of this bill remains, as evidenced by a *Guardian* investigation published in May 2021. While on the surface the new bill promises to protect landowners from anyone who intends to stay the night on the land they own, the *Guardian* identified forty-seven Facebook adverts bought by local Conservative candidates in the run-up to the May elections, seen at least 440,000 times, that specifically refer to how this bill will 'clean up' the filth of travelling sites. In a tactic used since the reign of Henry VIII, the rights of the general public have once again been restricted by manipulating bigotry against the travelling community.

It is important to stress that trespass in general has not been criminalised, that this new bill relates only to trespass with the intent to reside. It does not apply to swimming, rambling and all other forms of trespass, though of course the inevitable confusion that will stem from it will cause more people to feel that they are unwelcome in nature, that their presence causes some kind of new jeopardy. To be clear, it does not.

PUNISHMENT:

Under the new trespass offence, police will be permitted to seize vehicles and arrest any offenders, who will be liable for a fine of up to £2,500, and can be sentenced to up to three months in prison, or both.

THE SEMIOTICS OF TRESPASS

Trespass signs have deteriorated over the last century. You have to be very lucky these days to come across a decent sign while trespassing. Some 'private fishing' signs are still cast in metal, occasional woodland signs are hand-painted, but more often than not, the signs that forbid us access are either cheap, plasticated cardboard, similar to that of an estate agent's FOR SALE sign, or even worse, laminated printouts that bleed in the rain. The establishment aren't even trying any more.

In spite of what the law says, not all trespass is equal. The laws that prevent us from entering nuclear sites, just like the signs that warn us of a £1,000 fine for trespassing onto railway lines, serve the public interest. These signs are prohibitive for everyone's sake. Nobody wants to be involved in a rail collision any more than they do a nuclear incident. However, the laws and the signs of trespass to our rivers, forests and meadows of England are altogether different. They do not serve the public interest. Resting on years of precedent, and laws created by a parliament peopled entirely by landowners, they serve very few of us.

No one but lawyers actually sits down to read the letter of the

law, and unless they specialise in tort, even lawyers are hazy on the detail. The rest of us are governed by lines of legislation that we know almost nothing about, put off from nature by hearsay and, on the ground, signs. So the real effect on our experience of the countryside is not the law, but the way the law is represented – the branding of the countryside, the way it looks and the way that makes us feel.

For such a slight infraction of the law, it is quite stunning how much signage exists in the countryside. Where else can we find signs reminding us not to break the law? Houses don't have NO BURGLARY signs; pubs don't have NO BATTERY signs; clubs don't have NO MURDER signs. So why decorate the countryside with NO TRESPASSING signs? The signs are evidence of our

natural urge to ignore them; they appear where trespassers are most likely to be, insisting that what we do naturally is unnatural, against the stated order of the place. The signs are there to ward us off, but collectively they have a further effect, one that goes deep into our psyche. They construct a contrived reality, a hallucination that is desperate to persuade us away from our natural instinct, that insists we don't belong in nature.

Semiotics is the study of signs and symbols and how society interprets them, and is therefore an appropriate lens through which to view trespass. It maps our cultural associations with aesthetics, from typeface to music, from advertising to propaganda. It is used to develop branding strategies and marketing campaigns, but it is also useful for performing a living autopsy on the orthodoxies of culture: it investigates things that we take for granted and it lifts the hood on consensus. It explains, for example, how and why Tom Cruise looks so cool wearing sunglasses in *Top Gun*. Semiotics is fascinated by the process in which a basic tool for shading the eyes has somehow earned social capital associated with attractiveness and power, and it does this by delving into the mechanics of what makes things 'sexy' or 'cool' by unpacking the connotations we have with objects and how our response to them is influenced by a myriad of interconnected social factors.

We can look at trespass through the same prism. Trespass signs are more often than not set in capital letters, whose semiotics convey seriousness, importance and urgency. Many are in red, a colour which is used (across species) to convey danger, and some come with the familiar yellow-and-black colour scheme of building-site signage, implying there is serious work afoot.

Signs are frank statements, not conversation starters. They are already waiting for you when you arrive, which gives them a sense of rootedness, as if what they say has a more solid legitimacy than anything you, travelling through, might think. Many signs will be branded with an estate logo, often a heraldic coat of arms. Any logo serves to make us think their command has formality, that it is backed by a corporate body, an army of believers; the logo implies you are outnumbered. But when the logo is heraldic, the semiotics evoke a sense of history, as if the command is backed by knights of the round table, chivalric codes, men on horseback wielding swords.

The sartorial side of trespass, the tweed and guns of the landowning establishment, is also deeply associated with our notion of England. Tweed was a traditional weave invented in the

Outer Hebrides in the eighteenth century, but underwent a rebrand in the 1840s when Lady Gertrude Murray, Countess of Dunmore, introduced it to the British aristocracy, as hunting, shooting and fishing apparel. At the time of the Clearances (from the mid-eighteenth to the mid-nineteenth centuries), when local Scots were being evicted from their land to make way for English owners to farm sheep, Scots Gaelic was banned, folk music was outlawed and the traditional craft of *tweel* was appropriated and mispronounced by the imperialist, colonial impera-tives of the English, who wore their tweed like the skin of conquered

GET YOUR OWN
PRIVATE
WOODLAND

tribespeople. Tweed became the uniform of power, communicating a control over the land and, by extension, the people.

The semiotics of the countryside, from the signs, to the wire, to the uniforms, combine to make one clear message: it is not for us. This is a manipulative type of semiotics, a corporate branding exercise that allows those who own it to commodify it, rent it and profit from it, and to pretend that is the only way nature can be experienced. But the deeper effect is that it has changed the way we see the countryside, and ourselves within it. It has restructured our consciousness, filtered our senses, redesigned how we feel in nature: we look at the hills and woodland before us, and see the vista as a two-dimensional postcard, a flat picture, something that can never be entered, only observed from a suitable distance.

But remove the trespass signs, eliminate the law that forbids us access, reframe the semiotics, and suddenly we see the countryside as a three-dimensional possibility – something to be experienced. A river invites its swimmers, a tree invites its climbers, the frozen landscape thaws and becomes not a thing, but a process, a continuous interrelation of living things – motion, mobility, ever-changing experience. All of which leads us into another field of study: the study of how we experience the outside world, or *phenomenology*.

PHEASANTS
NOT
PEASANTS

Jon Moses

Doctor of phenomenology

I grew up in South Wales on the Gwent Levels, an old marshland drained by the Romans to create a breadbasket to fuel their invasion. My first relationship with nature was in that unusual space, a frontier landscape which felt wild and unregulated. It was only later I realised how unusual that was. Having grown up roaming there, to visit the rest of the countryside – regulated, managed, contained in little slices of access – came as a shock.

I now live in the Monnow Valley. It's a stunning place, but my capacity to access it without a car at hand is very limited. I can walk along the local river for two or three minutes before I get diverted away onto roads by fencing. When you're forced to stick to the roads or the pathways, your experience of nature is very passive; it privileges the visual sense over all others. You become an observer of nature, not a part of it. To experience nature, to feel that sense of belonging, I have to trespass.

We now think that our consciousness functions by first producing predictions about the world which are then error-checked by our sensory inputs. Reality is a kind of edited compromise between these competing data points; what the neuroscientist Anil Seth calls a kind of 'controlled hallucination'. The result is that, for the most part, we live in a world curated by our own expectations – or those of others. Without powerful, fresh experiences to act as a corrective, we remain trapped in a prison of our predictions. The world becomes less vibrant, less capable of inserting itself into the reservoir of our consciousness, and we spend more time sitting in the mental room marked out for self-rumination. The enclosure of the landscape, which keeps us hemmed into a few designated rights of way, is the perfect outer expression of this function. When we are forced onto the known path we are less likely to encounter spontaneity or surprise, and less plugged into the acquisition of new information about where we are. Familiarity begets insularity; our minds turn inward to ruminate on their preferred fixations.

Our depression crisis may well be a result of this overdominance of prediction. Depressives appear to spend more time stuck in a stance of consciousness called the 'default mode network' – a space for idle mental rumination, activated when we're not engaged in making any executive demands. Our well-being is battered by the narrow horizons of this selfhood, leaving us in a spiral of ruminative, obsessive thoughts. In time, these thoughts furrow the neural network, with the result that we 'become' what we think we are. The world does not simply feel less vibrant to the depressive mind, it becomes so. The resolution of experience has been dialled down. Our relationship with space trains us to just pass through it. We look at the map, plot our walk from A to B, and though we might stop for sandwiches, we pass through the natural world as tourists. For many years that's how I experienced the landscape as well, trapped in this convention of transience, trained always to observe from a distance, never to investigate the world on a deeper level. Once the capacity to investigate is, quite literally, shut off from us, the instinct to investigate withers too.

Recently I've tried to change that mindset, 'unseeing' the fence and reigniting my instinct to explore. But there's no getting around the fact that, at first, such trespassing alters your neurology. Stepping over the line marked 'private' comes with a spike of adrenalin, putting you in a state of hyperawareness. You're not tuning into the landscape but on the lookout for threat. But the more I force myself to attend to tiny details – perhaps lichens, or the fungi in the grass – the more that feeling diminishes. Our attentive capacity is limited and we can choose the inputs we use to fill it. And the more we attend to those details of the land, the better we know it and the more we start to feel we belong to it, or even begin to hold some kind of informal proprietorship over it. I document the flora I find, clear up rubbish and start to understand the way it interacts. And that subverts the hierarchy written into the place. When I'm challenged about what I'm doing on private land, I simply reply: looking after it.

THE ART OF TRESPASS

Trespass is easy. It simply means doing anything on land while not owning it. Walking, swimming, painting, singing, camping, snoozing, checking your phone – it's all trespass if you don't own the land you're doing it on. We'll look into what can actually be done on land and water later on in this companion, but first, we'll focus on the hardest element of trespass: crossing the boundary.

The Way of the Badger

When confronted with barbed wire, often the easiest approach is to slip beneath the lower wire and the ground. Barbed wire is often loosely swathed, so it's useful to find a small Y-shaped stick to place under the wire, lifting it up, allowing you to slip underneath. Often you will find a smoot or a smeuse, a burrow that has been formed by animals over years of constant use; this will usually give you a couple of inches of extra space, and allows you to

literally go the way of the badger. In fact, while we're at it, badger paths are by far the best way to cut through woodland; you won't be disturbing rare flowers or delicate ecosystems if you're following paths that have already been flattened by the heavy, pendulous backside of a badger, a species seemingly unconcerned with the conservation status of a landscape.

The Way of the Deer

This might seem like the most graceful approach, but unless you can leap through the air like a roe deer, going over a fence often exposes your crotch to the potential snag of barbed wire. Trying to unpin your gusset from a coil of barbed wire while perched halfway over a fence tends to bring you down to earth.

But fear not, there are usually plenty of natural aids available.

Walk the perimeter of the fence to see what nature has provided. Sometimes great oak trees come crashing down, crushing the fence, crumbling the wall, forming a handy wooden bridge into the forbidden land. At other times, great coppices of hazel sprout from interdicted land, over the wire, into your hands; they can be used as climbing frames. The corners of fences are similarly useful; there is often a diagonal strut to support the post, which also acts as a platform for your boots. But remember, whatever you do, don't damage the fence: aside from being rude, it counts as criminal damage.

If no such option is available, then your local hardware

merchants may have the answer: a foldable stool should set you back little more than a fiver. About half a foot high, they can be placed underneath the fence, half in, half out, allowing the trespasser to scissor-step over the top, from one side of the stool to the other. These lightweight stools also double as handy seats on rainy days, making them indispensable to the modern trespasser.

The Way of the Otter

Very often, rivers are protected with the most lethal defences of all: a combination of razor wire and an especially vicious style of barricade called triple-point palisade security fencing, the kind you'll find around electricity generators. That the single most gentle, peaceful components of the English landscape are adorned with such ugly violence is a crime itself against aesthetics. But to climb these fences is to slice one's body into fleshy ribbons and is only ever attempted by migrants at militarised borders, with the aid of mattresses and duvets as protection. It is often worth approaching these fences, gently touching the spikes at the top, and contemplating the level of desperation that forces humans to take themselves over the top.

So, instead, go the way of the otter. These zones of impenetrable razor fencing only last as long as

the private fishing rights to the river, so find a place further upstream, slip into the water and swim. Be careful, however, to work out in advance where you will leave the river; to be trapped inside forbidden ground is a surreal and slightly scary experience, especially when exhausted through exercise.

The Way of the Sycamore

Parachuting into private land, like a sycamore seed floating on the wind, is not for everyone. However, for certain areas of open-access land in England, it is the only way to get there. These places, including various sites on the South Downs, are called 'open-access islands', and are the result of bog-standard poor planning. They are areas of land on which the public has the right to roam; however, there are no rights of way to take us there. The only

feasible way to get into them is to trespass – or to parachute from such a great height that you won't be done for trespassing airspace (though this height is undefined by law).

But by far the largest, most difficult boundary to cross is the one in your own head. After a thousand years of manipulated semiotics, the conception that we are committing a crime by walking in woodland or swimming in a river is so strong that it can be hard to overcome. Get over that, and you can get over pretty much any wall.

REWILD YOUR WALKING BOOTS:

TRESPASS

WHERE TO TRESPASS

Our Water

As we've seen, 97 per cent of English rivers are out of bounds to the public. This is great news for the trespasser, because to trespass on water in England, you have only a 3 per cent chance of failure. Likewise, there are about 2,000 reservoirs in England, most of which are out of bounds.

The benefit of rivers and reservoirs is not just their peaceful, health-giving properties, but the fact that they are often so accessible. However, our lack of access rights mean these valuable resources cannot be used. For example, the area encompassing Liverpool, Manchester, Leeds, Sheffield and Doncaster has more than 250 reservoirs, but a distinct lack of free, open-access swim spots. The 7.6 million people who live in this area are effectively banned from the benefits of wild swimming. What is even more bizarre is that reservoirs have a statutory obligation to provide for public access. Section 3 (5) of the Water Industry Act (1991) states that water companies must 'ensure that the water or land is made available for recreational purposes and is made available in the best manner'. While many reservoirs have footpaths and provisions for fishing and boating, swimming, kayaking and paddleboarding are generally neglected. Likewise, an area of the River Loddon in Hampshire, a resource that could serve the public health needs of 110,000 people in Basingstoke, is reserved for just eighty fishermen, who claim the legal right to exclusivity even though many of their members live abroad. Swimmers, kayakers and paddleboarders are evicted by bailiffs to keep the riverbank empty, just in case members might want to fish there in private.

To add to the bizarre relationship the law creates between the public and open water, swimming is *specifically banned* on open-access land. Under the CRoW Act, our access rights extend only to certain types of 'open-air recreation', none of which include swimming, kayaking or paddleboarding. In fact, to do any of these on open-access land redefines our presence as an act of trespass, and if caught, we lose the right of access for seventy-two hours. It is hard to know exactly what happened to water access rights during the discussions leading to the CRoW Act, but a report from the *Guardian* in April 2000, eight months before the bill was passed, hints at how they might have been sacrificed in the process of compromise:

> **Any attempt to extend the controversial right to roam legislation will be opposed by landowners and the Conservatives, who last week faced accusations of trying to wreck the bill after tabling 138 amendments limiting its provisions ... Privately, ministers are warning campaigners that the bill has always been a 'project of negotiations and compromises'.**

When the time comes to extend our rights of access, the process will again, inevitably, be one of compromise against forceful opposition from the lobby groups of orthodox exclusion. This time, though, access to our blue spaces must be at the core of our new rights to land.

English woodland is central to the English imagination of itself.
Shakespeare's fictional Arden in *A Midsummer Night's Dream*, Robin
Hood's Sherwood Forest, the woodland that inspired Roald Dahl's *Fantastic
Mr Fox* (Jones Hill Wood, most of which has recently been razed to
the ground by the High Speed Two/HS2 rail project) – our woods are
warehouses of inspiration. They also nurture more wildlife than any
other habitat in the country, providing homes for thousands of species of
mammals, birds, reptiles and invertebrates. Not only this, English woods
are home to almost half of the bluebells in the world.

And yet, England is one of the least wooded nations in Europe. Europe's
average woodland cover is 44 per cent, but in England we have a meagre
10 per cent. This figure falls to only 2 per cent if we're talking about ancient
woodland, whose invaluable soil structure has remained intact for almost
five centuries.

But we are allowed entry to so few of them: nearly three-quarters of the
UK's woodland is privately owned, and a third of it by only a thousand
individuals. According to Guy Shrubsole at whoownsengland.org, 'The
vast majority comprise large and ancient aristocratic estates – two dukes,
two earls, a marquess, a viscount and two barons – whose families and
landholdings go back a very long way.' Though much of this woodland is
eligible for public subsidies (in other words, financed by the taxpayer) the
public is barred from it. Only 16.2 per cent of people in the UK have access
to a wood of at least two hectares within 500 metres of their home. An
additional 37 per cent of the UK's population would have a local accessible
wood if access rights were given to existing woods. During the debates
before the CRoW Act, some MPs proposed amendments that would have
extended our right to roam over woodlands and riverbanks, but they were
opposed by pro-shooting lobby groups such as the Countryside Alliance
and never made it into law.

So to this day, we remain excluded from woodland for the same reason William the Conqueror (England's great-grandfather of exclusion) evicted people from his forests nearly a thousand years ago: hunting. Today, English woodlands are used as green marquees for the breeding of pheasants, 47 million of which are released into the countryside every year. We are banned because it is claimed we would disturb their breeding, and because when people pay to shoot them, we might also be shot. The question is whether the right to breed and exterminate birds should override the public's right to healthcare. Bluntly, it should not.

Our Green Belts

Green belts are areas of countryside that surround urban zones, created to prevent the spread and eventual amalgamation of towns and cities. They take up only 13 per cent of land in England, and yet are perhaps the most important area of open space to the public, because so many of us live within easy access of them. If green belts were opened up to responsible public access, the 30 million people living near them would have better access to outdoor recreation and the mental and physical health benefits that come with this.

The 2021 National Planning Policy Framework stipulates that local planning authorities should plan 'positively to enhance the beneficial use of the Green Belt, such as looking for opportunities to provide access; to provide opportunities for outdoor sport and recreation; to retain and enhance landscapes, visual amenity and biodiversity; or to improve damaged and derelict land'. However, today only 3.9 per cent of the green belt is open-access land, which is 7 per cent of the total open-access land in Britain. When the science clearly demonstrates that our health is improved by regular immersion in nature, green belt land, the very nature on our doorsteps, should be a priority in extending the CRoW Act.

If the public were allowed full access to our green belts, perhaps they might have more reason to protect them. The government's own data shows that there has been a 62 per cent increase in the loss of greenfield green belt (land that has never been built on before) since 2013, with 315 hectares lost in 2016–17 alone. The Campaign to Protect Rural England (CPRE) released a report in 2021 that showed how pressures on our precious green belt land have quadrupled since 2013. The 'State of the Green Belt' report shows that at this moment there are a quarter of a million homes planned to be built on green-belt land – a rise of 475 per cent since 2013.

About two-thirds of green-belt land is agricultural, and home to many of the remaining hedges that support so much of our wildlife. Hedge cover has halved since the end of the Second World War, but our green belt, which contains hedgerows that have been there since the Middle Ages, provides a sanctuary for nature. These hedges support a myriad of life, providing song posts, shelter and nesting opportunities for both woodland and farmland birds.

As long as people respect the fact that much of this land is an agricultural workplace, as long as we abide by the rules of the Countryside Code, there is no reason that we cannot follow the Scottish model and be granted access to our most accessible countryside.

Our Council Land

Local authorities own around 1.3 million acres of land in England, making them collectively a very significant set of landowners. There are councils in England that own moorlands, saltmarshes, large areas of green belt and even vast expanses of foreshore – not to mention scores of golf courses.

Much of this land was bought in the early 1920s to protect it from development, and the money that purchased it, of course, came from council rates – from the public purse. If the public collectively bought this land, then why are we not allowed the automatic rights of access that come with ownership?

On 24 July 2021, some three hundred local Sussex residents trespassed one such area of council property on the South Downs. The Landscapes of Freedom trespass highlighted that of the 12,500 acres of land owned by Brighton and Hove Council, locals have the right to access only 10 per cent of it. The particular plot of land they trespassed was rented by a farmer, who used it, once again, as a pheasant shoot. Other than the organisers, not one of the locals present at the trespass had ever been to that land or even realised it was there.

It is not easy to find out what land near you is council-owned. The UK companies dataset that the Land Registry started publishing in November 2017 offers a spreadsheet of addresses, but it doesn't include any maps. This is useful in locating disused urban land but next to useless for rural land, where the boundaries might stretch far and wide. In 2011, then communities secretary Eric Pickles commissioned what he called the 'First Public Property Map' to demonstrate the 'sheer scale and variety of public sector asset wealth' and encourage councils to 'take a good hard look at what they own'. Sadly, the public can't see it because Pickles' department only published the map for a year or so before taking it down. There remains no central map of council land, but this information can be gleaned from individual councils through Freedom of Information (FOI) requests. When you consider that you have helped to buy council land and that you continue to subsidise it, trespassing there doesn't seem much like trespassing at all.

Our Golf Courses

During the first national lockdown in 2020, when the streets and parklands of our cities and towns were crowded with people taking their allocated exercise, the Right to Roam movement campaigned for golf courses to be opened up to the public. Based on research conducted by the campaign, *The Times* published some very striking statistics: if all 3,087 of Britain's golf courses were opened to the public, they would provide over a million more people with easy access to green space ('easy access' was defined as being within a 500-metre walk).

An average eighteen-hole golf course in the UK takes up 150 acres of green space, making them much larger than most public parks, and they are often situated deep in the heart of urbanised zones, the only patch of green in a desert of grey concrete. There are 481,000 acres of public green space in Britain and about 311,000 acres of golf courses, meaning that opening up the links to public access would increase our access to green space by two-thirds. This statistic was particularly resonant during lockdown, when people taking exercise in urban zones were finding it increasingly difficult to maintain social distancing. The report said, 'In the unlikely event that every Briton took to the nation's golf courses simultaneously and were evenly spaced, each would have nearly 210 square feet in which to self-isolate.' Of course, the golfing community hit back. They claimed that 'not all golf clubs are in a position to allow the general public on their courses, due to wildlife management programmes that protect wildflowers and bees'. There is some gumption in this statement, not least because golf greens, with their neat, weeded lawns, are a man-made desert of biodiversity, and, excepting supermarket car parks, they couldn't look less like an ideal habitat for bees. The pesticides used in maintaining a golf green not only starve our pollinating bees of habitat, but are used in such quantities that they fill the air and pose a health threat to neighbouring humans. The greenwashing of designating select areas of golf courses for growing wild flowers might work for brochures and government targets, but it is a negligible factor when assessing the public's need for open space.

The real, unspoken argument against opening up golf courses to public access is that it would undermine the age-old privilege that comes with private property: exclusivity. But when almost 25,000 Birmingham residents and 17,000 in both Solihull and Bolton would benefit from opening up golf courses in their areas, the question remains: why should the exclusivity of these courses override the public's right to the benefits of open space? The question becomes even more relevant when you realise how many of these golf courses are owned by local councils. In Greater London there are 130 golf courses, covering 11,000 acres of space, and almost half are owned by local councils.

Caversham Heath golf course near Reading was one of a select few clubs that did opt to open up their courses during lockdown. Residents of a neighbouring care home were allowed onto the land to take their daily exercise, providing a temporary experiment in how open access to golf courses would work. A club official quoted in *Golfing Times* sounded surprised that the public hadn't torn up the turf and burned down the club house: 'It's quite strange for our members, but they see that people are respecting the property. These are exceptional times and our members were keen to help the community.'

In Scotland, thanks to the Land Reform Act of 2003, all golf courses are open access. Golfers play alongside local residents taking exercise, and both parties have learned how to coexist, to share the resource of open space; the Scottish access laws encourage both parties to be respectful of each other's needs. To trespass the golf courses in England is to question how land is used and who it is used for.

Our Crown Land

Crown land is the name given to four categories of ownership: land belonging to the monarch (the Crown Estate), the private property of the monarch (such as the Sandringham estate), land belonging to the duchies (the Duchy of Lancaster and the Duchy of Cornwall) and government land.

The Crown Estate is a collection of rural land and urban property that extends to almost 300,000 acres of land in the UK, with a total worth of over £14 billion. Unlike the Duchy of Lancaster (the private estate of the Queen) and the Duchy of Cornwall (the private land of Prince Charles), the Crown Estate is 'the sovereign's public estate', meaning it is owned neither by the government nor by the monarch per se, but by Britain itself. However, all but 15 per cent of the profit made by the estate is given to the Treasury, meaning the public benefit from its wealth, and yet we are still banned from setting foot on it.

The Queen's private ownership of Sandringham comes to some 8,000 acres of Norfolk; the Duchy of Lancaster covers 46,000 acres, most of which is made up of rural estates in Lancashire, Yorkshire, Cheshire, Staffordshire and Lincolnshire; while the Duchy of Cornwall stretches over 131,000 acres of land, dotted across twenty-six counties, mostly across south-west England.

To open up the majority of Crown land to public access (obviously not

including private gardens and sites that are sensitive for security or ecological reasons) would send a powerful message to the landowning elite of England. The monarch is still the top dog of the aristocracy, and the Crown Estate is one of the most successful land-management schemes in the country. If the Crown dedicated its land to public access under the CRoW Act, it would dispel that age-old aristocratic barrier to public access, which pretends it is an issue of class envy and not public health. What with the work that Princes William and Harry have been doing to promote mental health issues, the Crown could do nothing more proactive for the mental health of its subjects than opening up its land under the CRoW Act. Plus, 'Put the CRoW into the Crown' is a catchy slogan.

TAKE ACTION FOR ACCESS

If you're new to trespassing, first of all don't worry, there is very little jeopardy. To be absolutely certain of where you stand in the law, check out the information provided by Green and Black Cross, an voluntary organisation of lawyers who provide legal advice and help for people engaged in protest and direct action (greenandblackcross.org, search for 'trespass').

Turn the trespass into a heist movie: meet up with your friends, get the maps out, research the area you want to trespass, understand the historical context of the land, and find out who owns it and what it is used for (more details on this can be found in the chapter 'Going Deeper into the Land').

'The more that people experience the land, the more they understand it, the more they will love it and feel part of it like we farmers do. It's that old adage, 'You can't love what you don't know.'

ROMILLY SWANN, SHEEP FARMER

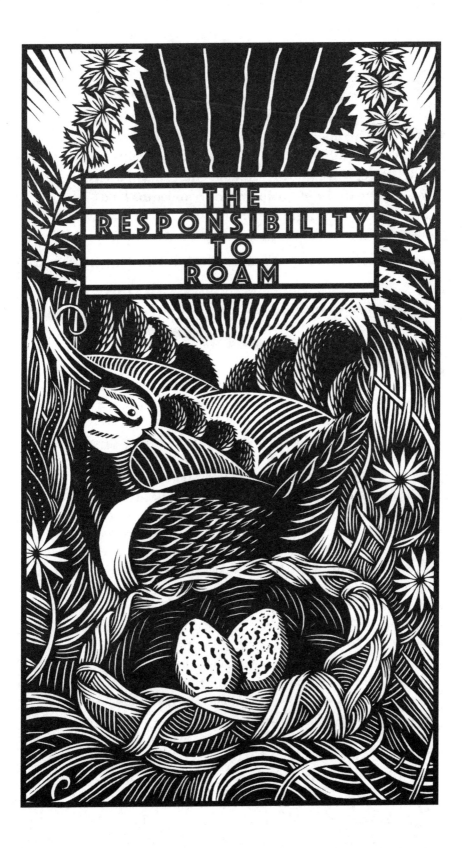

THE RESPONSIBILITY TO ROAM

T he right to roam is an ancient contract between the land and the people. It existed long before state legal systems, long before government and long before nations. It has various iterations across Europe, each nation defining it slightly differently from any other, and only relatively recently has it been codified into law. Among other localised specifics, it gives anyone the right to explore and wander the land and the waterways, and the right to sleep out beneath the stars. And it states our responsibilities in so doing. It is a code of connection.

The right to roam emerged out of a culture of land use that existed long before private property: the commons (we will explore this further in the next chapter). The right for people to access land they don't own is the last thread of the fabric of a wider commons philosophy, a network of codes and reciprocal relationships of care between communities and nature that was torn to shreds by the process of enclosure. It is a time capsule from a world that was more connected to nature, and for that reason, it is cherished by the nations that embrace it, who regard it as a monument of national heritage.

In England, not much is known about the right to roam. Those financially fortunate enough to have holidayed among the Norwegian fjords or the forests of Finland will have tasted its freedom, and possibly read the codes of conduct, but apart from that, our knowledge of the actual ins and outs of what a right to roam means is concealed behind a wall of propaganda erected by the landowning lobby. The most common argument against extending our access rights in England actually has nothing to do with the tenets of a right to roam, and is premised on the contrived assumption that it encourages the absolute abolition of privacy. The argument is often expressed as a rhetorical question, which goes something like this: 'I suppose you wouldn't mind me invading your back garden, then?' This statement is often presented as a masterful, game-changing chess move that will checkmate even the most ardent right-to-roam campaigner. But it is a ludicrous proposition – that campaigners are openly encouraging home invasion, seeking to set up their tents in people's rockeries and wild swim in their fish ponds.

It is irrational, and yet, given the centuries of English law that we have internalised, quite reasonable. English law does not differentiate between jumping the fence into someone's suburban back garden and walking in thousands of acres of deciduous woodland. It maintains the legal fiction that pretends these two acts are of equal consequence, and wilfully ignores the elements of scale and context that make swimming in a river manifestly different from sleeping in a stranger's garden.

THE RIGHT TO ROAM IN EUROPE

Property law in England imagines the rights of an owner to be a 'bundle of sticks'. When you buy the property, you are buying a bundle of rights: the right to build on the land, the right to mine it, the right to take rent from it, and in England, since William the Conqueror imported the notion from Normandy, the right to exclude others. Writing in 1766, jurist William Blackstone described this right as the principal foundation of private property, 'that sole and despotic dominion which one man claims and exercises over the external things of the world, in total exclusion of the right of any other individual in the universe'. But in countries that have a more expansive right to roam than ours, there are still large landowners, there are counts and lords and companies who own much of the country. It's just that their rights of ownership are balanced against the public need to access nature.

Another myth of the right to roam is that it encourages a free-for-all, that it is a golden ticket to do whatever you like on someone else's property.

Again, this is an outrageous postulation: that there should be laws that specifically encourage crimes against nature and society, as long as they are committed on private property. Each right-to-roam tradition across Europe is actually a series of codes and practices that demand responsibility from the walker or swimmer, codes that ensure respect for the ecology of the landscape and for the business of the landowner, not to mention the rest of the community of human and non-human creatures that live there. So little is known of the exact elements of the right to roam that the myth of public invasion persists in England. So, to begin chipping away at the wall of fiction, we'll begin by taking a look at some of the other rights to roam out there.

Norway

The traditional Norwegian code of *allemannsretten* (every person's right) first draws a clear distinction between *innmark* ('infield', land inside the boundaries), which is reserved for private use, and *utmark* ('outfield', land outside the boundaries), which covers everything else. In practice, *utmark* will be the main parts of beaches, bodies of water, bogs, heaths, forests and mountains in Norway – areas that are uncultivated and undeveloped. The Outdoor Activities Act 1957 specifically defined *innmark* as 'courtyard, house plot, cultivated land, meadows, cultivated pastures and forest plantations and similar areas where public traffic will be unduly congested for owner or user'.

To protect *innmark*, Norway has created a legal buffer zone between outside and inside, with campers

and roamers not allowed to come within 150 metres of private property. Campfires are allowed, but not in forest areas between 15 April and 15 September, unless you're camping in a place where it obviously can't lead to a larger fire (a pebble beach, for example). When camping, you can stay overnight without the express permission of the landowner, but you have to move on after a day.

The first principle for maintaining the right of public access in Norway is consideration and caution, 'so that no damage is done and does not cause inconvenience, neither to the landowner nor others'. This caution places specific emphasis on considerations for vulnerable flora and fauna – pointing to seasonal fluctuations, such as flowering, breeding and nesting seasons – but also on landowners' requirements, seeding, harvesting and so on. The Norwegian right to roam protects the rights of landowners alongside the rights of the public.

Finland

Around 96 per cent of Finland's land areas are accessible under the code of *jokamiehenoikeudet*, which has a similar meaning to *allemannsretten* in Norway. Exceptions to this right include nature conservation sites, construction sites or areas of land dedicated to national defence. The Finnish code is essentially a list of the things you are forbidden from doing – a list of important safeguards that protect the landowner and the nature of the area. To list just a few: you are forbidden from disturbing the use of land by the landowner, moving about in yards, cultivated areas or cultivated fields, cutting down or harming growing trees, taking moss or lichen, disturbing domestic premises, dropping litter, and disturbing or damaging birds' nests. Again, these restrictions expand and contract in relation to the specific ecology of the area and the seasonal changes.

Key to the Finnish right to roam is the statement, 'Every person's rights are public, and every person residing in Finland enjoys them, regardless of their citizenship.' The right applies to everyone on the land, and as such has become a key factor in tourism. The countryside is a national asset, and like Finland's oil reserves or its traditional cultural practices, generates a significant proportion of its national wealth.

Bavaria

The right to roam is so important in Bavaria it has been written into its constitution. The Constitution of Bavaria guarantees everyone 'the enjoyment of natural beauty and recreation in the outdoors, in particular the access to forests and mountain meadows, the use of waterways and lakes and the appropriation of wild fruits'. It is interesting that this specific article of the constitution lists the state's responsibilities to public access alongside its obligations to care for art, culture and historical monuments. This tells us a great deal about how Bavarians view their rights to nature: it is inherent to the culture of their state, an essential component of what it means to be Bavarian. This specific right even has a nickname, which shows how well known and beloved it is among Bavarian society. *Schwammerlparagraph* ('the mushroom clause') refers specifically to the right to forage, which is considered an essential component of interacting with

nature and represents the ideology of our rights to nature: to pick mushrooms, more than anything else, requires a detailed knowledge of nature. The constitution also obliges 'every person to treat nature and the landscape with care'.

Scotland

Scotland has, in some ways, the most liberating and radical approach to public access across all of Europe. It allows a general right of public access to most areas of land and water, and specifies three types of activity that are licensed: recreational purposes (including wild camping, kayaking, wild swimming, horse riding, mountain biking and rambling), carrying out relevant educational activities (citizen science, school programmes, etc.) and limited types of commercial activities. You have the right to light a fire, with sensible considerations of context, and you have the right to forage.

These rights of access are limited, as with all other right-to-roam codes, by the usual reasonable exceptions. These include:

- houses and other private residences (and sufficient space around them);
- land where crops are growing, though you are still allowed access to field margins;
- land which is next to or used by a school;

- places that charge for entry, such as visitor attractions;
- land on which building or engineering works are being carried out, or which is being used for mineral working or quarrying;
- land set out for a particular recreational purpose, such as sports fields, golf greens, tennis courts or bowling greens.

Like all right-to-roam traditions in Europe, Scotland's rights depend on responsible access. But they have gone out of their way to make these codes of responsibility clear and well disseminated. The Scottish Outdoor Access Code strips the paint of the English Countryside Code. It is a detailed description of the responsibilities you owe not just

the land but also the communities, workers and owners associated with it. For all its no-stone-unturned detail, it can be summarised with its three core principles: respect the interests of others, care for the environment, and take responsibility for your own actions.

And, as with all public-facing messaging campaigns, it's not just the content, but the style of information dissemination that counts. Google the Scottish Outdoor Access Code and explore their website: notice the usability, the bright colours, the photography, the design and the tone, all of which contribute to making it a resource that is much more likely to actually be used, to actually be effective.

And then, just for fun, search for England's Countryside Code. The difference is stark, laughable even. The Scottish Outdoor Access Code is an information machine for the twenty-first century; the English Countryside Code is a clown's car with square wheels and bubbles coming out of the exhaust. If England really wants people to engage with the countryside responsibly, it's going to have to move its education format from the chalkboard to the iPhone.

RULES FOR THE GUEST

The Finnish right to roam
from visitfinland.com

When you are on private land, remember that you are not only a guest in nature, but a guest of the landowner. You may wander freely and swim, cycle, canoe, go hook-and-line or ice fishing and even set up a tent for the night in some places, but use your best judgement and respect the privacy and rights of others too. Don't camp too close to a home or venture into private gardens.

Avoid excessive noise and take care not to disturb any local wildlife. Don't collect mosses, lichens and plant life that should stay where they belong and, most importantly, leave zero waste and no human footprint behind. The Finnish have zero tolerance to noise and littering in their beloved nature – be like a Finn and respect the land and its inhabitants.

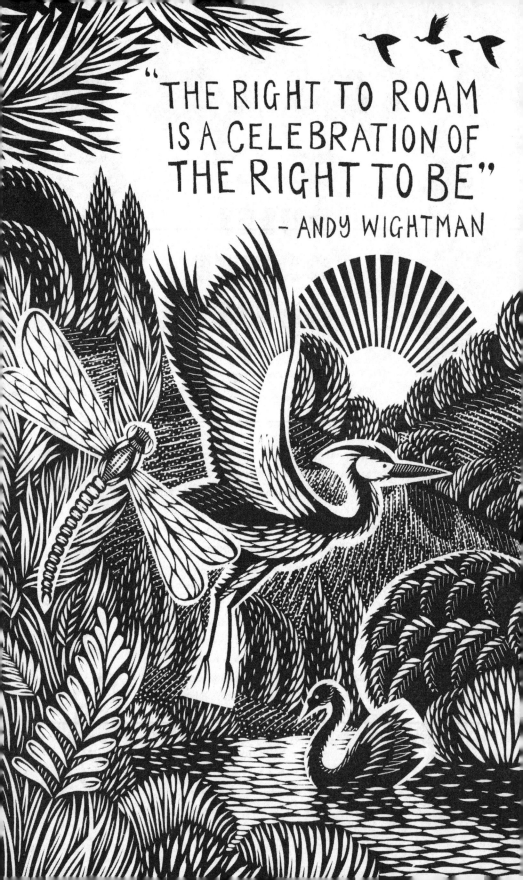

"THE RIGHT TO ROAM
IS A CELEBRATION OF
THE RIGHT TO BE"
- ANDY WIGHTMAN

Romilly Swann

Sheep farmer and natural dyer

I've looked after animals my whole life. I grew up on a smallholding, just a couple of acres on the south coast of England. We kept goats, chickens, ducks and geese, and we'd let neighbours graze their sheep and horses on our land too. I now keep a flock of about thirty Shetland sheep. I know each and every one of them, and they know me. It's much more than keeping stock – it's a relationship; they're like family members.

Alongside my commitments with the sheep, and my natural dyeing business, I keep goats, chickens and a small, shaggy workhorse, which are used therapeutically in my part-time work for Path Hill Outdoors, an organisation based on the Hardwick Estate in Oxfordshire that offers a one-to-one programme for kids that struggle with mainstream schooling. We take the children and go out into nature, find something to do – canoeing, carving, laying a fire, cuddling lambs – something from which they can gain a sense of fulfilment, to provide a space for connection with the natural environment and to each other.

For many years I worked at the Earth Trust, an environmental learning charity in Oxfordshire, where we educated kids in the outdoors. Alongside school day visits we ran a weekly programme for teenagers covering animal management, conservation and forestry skills. Through the seasons we'd hope that our students would learn practical rural skills alongside responsibility for themselves, each other and the environment. I have met many of them since who still love the outdoors and who used their experience with us to gain work in rural occupations such as tree surgery and the like.

Through a little club that some friends and I ran, each year we'd take up to twenty kids on a week-long camping walk somewhere beautiful, stopping at farms, knocking on doors and asking if they had a place we could pitch our tents for the night. We were almost universally met with amazing generosity and kindness. We'd guarantee our hosts that we'd leave no trace of our presence, and as a thank you we'd leave them a bottle of wine, chocolates or hand-drawn cards. We wanted to teach the kids to have faith in human hospitality. What happens when you knock on a stranger's door and ask for sanctuary? In the many years of exploring the countryside in this way, we must have been turned away only a couple of times.

I grew up around the River Cuckmere in East Sussex, in cider country. When the apple harvest came round, the whole village would turn out to bring in the harvest. Children would be playing in the farmers' barns, everyone would be there for the cracking of the barrels; it was a moment the whole community shared. Everyone knew who everyone was, and because we grew up in that environment, we internalised a powerful countryside code that was as much about respecting the community as the environment. I used to cut across farmland to get to school, and we used to play on private land all the time. No one would bother us, and if we saw something out of place, we would let the farmer know. We were the eyes and ears of the countryside.

But the thing is, to be helpful on the land, rather than a hindrance, you've got to know what you're seeing, you've got to understand the country. Back when I worked for the Earth Trust, we used to take kids out into the Sinodun Hills in Oxfordshire. At the foot of the hills, I'd give them my gate rant. I'd ask them to consider the most basic questions: Why is the gate here? What does it do? If it's open, why is that? If it's closed, why is that? So, we'd consider the dynamics of the gate, which would lead us to what work happened there, to walking safely among cows, explaining the context and the reasoning of the countryside. Then we'd all race to the top of the hill, with the whole Oxfordshire landscape rolling out beneath us, the river snaking off to the horizon, our hearts pumping, exhilarated. That's the way to learn about the countryside. It's that feeling of freedom, that bodily sense of liberation that's so important.

But if all of this leaves a trail of devastation, it's just not going to work. Dogs are a real issue. They can cause panic in a herd, and kill sheep more often than we like to think. But the public can be even more erratic and

unpredictable; they can do the weirdest stuff, things you just can't fathom.
BBQs and picnics in the middle of grazing fields; climbing gates and
breaking them instead of just opening and shutting them; parking in front
of gates, field entrances and tracks so that farmers can't get past; leaving all
sorts of unusual litter lying around. People think the problem with litter is
that it's just an eyesore, but it's much more serious than that. Just the other
day I had to have a lamb put down because he had ingested some plastic and
his digestive tract was blocked. Alan was his name. I helped birth Alan in
spring and then had to have him shot in the head, all for some careless act of
littering that meant nothing to the person that did it.

My field of sheep might as well be open-access land. It has four footpaths
running from the corners, and I meet people there all the time. I build up
relationships with them, and my sheep are almost famous in the local area;
they're friendly, gentle and curious to all passers-by. As long as people
respect my work and respect the animals, as long as they understand what's
going on, I don't have any problem at all with people being there. The more
that people experience the land, the more they understand it, the more they
will love it and feel part of it like we farmers do. It's that old adage, 'You can't
love what you don't know.'

WE'VE FORGOTTEN WHAT WE'VE LOST

In 2020, the Right to Roam campaign launched a petition against the criminalisation of trespass. We garnered 134,000 signatures and triggered a debate in parliament, a largely pointless pantomime of MPs' faces on Zoom, which took ages and got nothing done. But perhaps the most enlightening aspect of this charade was the map that accompanied the petition online, which showed where the signatures came from. A quick look revealed a striking conclusion: areas that were already well linked to nature were the areas most concerned with access to it.

This is no surprise. People with a healthy connection to nature realise, in their bones, how vital it is to their well-being and respond more energetically to the idea of it being taken away. If you went to Iceland now and put up Harris fencing around the rivers and lakes, there would be a national revolution. But here in England, we have grown used to our state of deprivation. Exclusion has become normalised; we've forgotten what we've lost.

We've already looked at the health benefits of greater access to nature, but a close reading of the right-to-roam codes in other countries reveals other, more nuanced, but no less important aspects that are harder to prove with science. There are significant ripple effects to a right to roam

– cultural benefits, improvements in child development, community cohesiveness and more – that are often overlooked in this debate.

The Swedes have an annual tradition called *sportlov* ('sports break'), which emerged from an energy crisis during the Second World War. Europe was running short of coal, causing the Swedish government to shut down schools for two weeks to save on energy. In order to keep the children occupied, ensuring their parents continued to go to work, the state offered outdoor activities instead. When the war was over, the government found that this holiday was so popular that they simply kept it going. These days, in the height of winter, schools shut down for a week every year so the children can go out into nature – with organised guides and activities, or if they're older, on their own – staying in cabins or camping, experiencing the outdoors. For Swedes, the outdoors is something to be experienced from a young age.

Swedish writers talk a lot about child development in nature; rather than being fenced off from the wild, hemmed in to someone else's boundaries, Swedes are blessed with the right to find their own limits. Tree climbing, rock leaping, river swimming, these activities are not just recreation, as defined in England, but are instead key components to a person's understanding of themselves (and it's better for everyone if this happens before the onset of adulthood).

Connecting with nature teaches responsibility – just ask the bushcraft community, the men and women who run courses on living in the out-side world. Using knives, billhooks and axes, washing up together, the

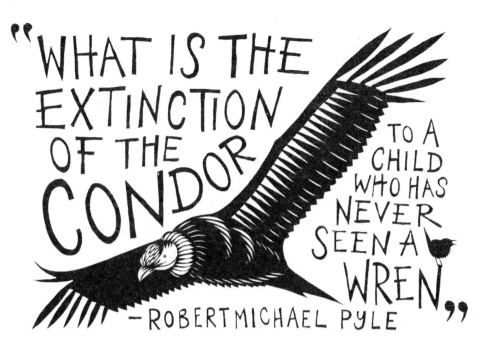

"WHAT IS THE EXTINCTION OF THE CONDOR TO A CHILD WHO HAS NEVER SEEN A WREN."

—ROBERT MICHAEL PYLE

celestial satisfaction of a bow-drilled fire, these skills teach you things you simply can't find in the classroom. But in England, you either have to rely on your parents to pay for these experiences, or misbehave so consistently at school that you are excluded and thus qualify for state-funded courses. Children learn a raft of responsibility by being in nature – responsibility for the tools they use, for the land they are in and to the people they share the experience with. Social responsibility can be taught in nature.

Recently, the Norwegian concept of *hygge*, referring to the cosy indoor fun to be had during winter, has taken root in England. But its counterpart, *friluftsliv*, is lesser known. The words were coined by Norwegian playwright and poet Henrik Ibsen in a poem written in 1859 called 'On the Heights', in which a farmer recounts his year spent in the wilderness and the joys and philosophy it brought him. The meaning of *friluftsliv* is something akin to our concept of mindfulness; it describes a deeper connection to the moment and to the landscape, a frame of mind that instils a deeper presence within oneself by experiencing a deeper connection to the world outside ourselves. It echoes the poet John Muir's famous quote about experiencing nature: 'By going out, I was really going in.' There is a power, a magnitude, a realism to what we experience

out there in nature that not only allows us to see ourselves clearly, but gives us the time and space to consider what to do about it.

In countries that have a right to roam, nature is not merely regarded as a pharmacy or a psychiatrist's couch. The connection is reciprocal, mutually beneficial, symbiotic. Emelie Thorngren, who organises children's activities for the Swedish Outdoor Association, the country's biggest non-profit outdoor sports organisation, says, 'The more people are given the opportunity to stay in nature, the more people want to protect it.' And there is science to back this up. A recent paper from the European Centre for Environment and Human Health at the University of Exeter suggests that people who have access to nature or urban green spaces are much more likely to behave in environmentally friendly ways. Dr Ian Alcock, who led the research, says, 'People who made more nature visits were more likely to engage in recycling and more likely to engage in green travel and were more likely to engage in environmental volunteering.' Using a representative sample of 24,000 people in England, researchers also found that the opposite is true, that people not exposed to green spaces were less likely to adopt green behaviours. It's useful to have the science to support what is basic human psychology:

we are much more able to empathise and care about something if we have had direct experience of it. With the disasters of climate change and habitat destruction so dishearteningly vast and abstract, it is useful to refocus our attention to the local as a way of connecting with the global. Or, as American scientist and poet Robert Michael Pyle wrote, 'What is the extinction of a condor to a child who has never seen a wren?'

But while we've forgotten what we've lost in terms of our mental health and our physical activity, we've also forgotten what we owe to nature. By breaking that bond between us and nature, by putting a barbed-wire fence between the human and the non-human, we've forgotten how to treat it, how to respect it, how to support it and how to ensure its sustainability. The total dominion given to a select few over our land has severed the sense that we all owe it our care, that we all have power to protect it. Our code of honour and respect for the countryside has withered on the vine because its roots have been cut.

TAKE ACTION FOR ACCESS

Read up on the right to roam, and since each country has a slightly different approach to it, consider what it might look like in England.

Visit the Scottish Outdoor Access Code online (outdooraccess-scotland.scot). In the absence of a useful code in England, adopt this one for your trespasses.

'The people around here are very protective of the land, so when the fracking came, or new developments, or the felling of trees, they banded together, showed solidarity and resisted. They defend what they love.'

JIM GHEDI, FOLK SINGER

Today there are still about one million acres of common land in England. These are pleasant areas, from a single acre to several hundred, and tend to be where locals take their exercise or walk their dogs. They might be wildflower meadows or wetlands designated Sites of Special Scientific Interest (SSSIs) and are often areas of sanctuary for rare species, but they are a shadow of what they once were, of how they were used, of what they really meant to people.

The commons were areas of land in which the locals, the commoners, had certain rights, including a de facto right of access. Each area of common ground had specific rights, which depended on the resource it offered. If it was a woodland, you could collect fallen wood for your fire; if the land was made of shale, you could mine it for building materials – all within parameters that were decided together by the local community. Each member of the community had rights to these features of the land, but only on the agreement that members work together to sustain the resource – it was an early philosophy of eco-sustainability, built around the idea that though none of them actually owned the land, they were caring for it in such a way that their grandchildren and their grandchildren's grandchildren could benefit from it too. Every year, commoners would vote in a 'reeve' to ensure this resource was not exploited.

The commons is not communism. The 'common' in common land refers not to shared ownership, but to rights that commoners held in privately owned land. The commons was a practical philosophy, a matrix of rights and responsibilities that balanced personal use with public responsibility, a traditional code that rested on the idea that certain resources were so essential to the public that in spite of being owned privately, they should be managed collectively. In his recent book *The Plunder of the Commons* Guy Standing shows how this culture can be applied throughout modern society, extending from where it began in land to more abstract public amenities such as health, air quality and law, all of which have suffered under the imposed culture of privatisation.

The culture of the commons is one of inclusivity: it is based on the idea that everyone has a need for certain resources, and that it follows that everyone should have a right to these resources, under strict guidelines that made sure they remained sustainable. Central to the idea of the commons was the phrase 'by reason of vicinage', which is old-fashioned speak for *because you're local*. It didn't matter who you were, or how much money you had: if you lived in the area, and contributed to its health and subsistence, you had rights in it.

THE ENCLOSURE OF COMMONS CULTURE

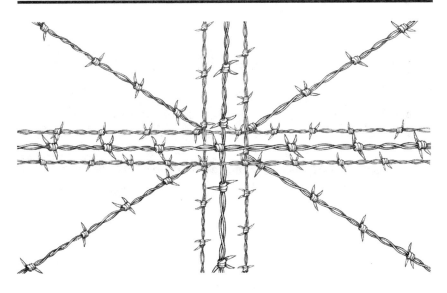

With the Norman invasion of 1066 came a new concept: enclosure. William the Conqueror and his barons put up palisades around large areas of common land to facilitate their desire to breed and hunt deer, enforcing a new law of exclusion with brutal violence. When common land turned into private land, it not only had the right of common access removed in favour of exclusive ownership, but took the wealth of the land from the locals and funnelled it into the pockets of a single individual, with no limits to their right to exploit it. While one man in the area got richer and richer, the rest of the commoners – men, women and children (now without their rights to winter fuel, building materials and pasture) – found they could no longer survive off the land.

Enclosure removed the right of the poor to self-subsistence. It robbed people of their autonomy. It funnelled them into the cities, desperate for work, fuelled the Industrial Revolution and turned the vast majority of the English into wage slaves. Protest, too, changed its focus, from resisting enclosure, fighting for our rights to the land, to bartering with management for workers' rights. It also took away the commoners' right to protect nature from exploitation,

HISTORIC RIGHTS OF COMMON

The Right of Estovers

The right to collect windfall wood for personal use. A size limit of an average arm's length was usual, and you were allowed enough for personal use only.

The Right of Pannage

The right to graze your pigs on beechmast. A good example of localised rights, for those who lived near beechwoods.

The Right of Turbary

The right to dig the earth for minerals, shale or slate. Turbary refers specifically to peat, which was dried and roasted to heat the home.

The Right of Piscary

The right to fish in the waters of common land. Locals would monitor fish stocks and make sure everyone kept to the limit of personal use.

The Right of Brakes

The right to cut down brake (otherwise known as bracken) and heather for the principal purpose of bedding down livestock in winter.

The Right of Shack

The right to let livestock wander through fields after harvest to feed on the leftovers – this was most prevalent in Norfolk, Lincoln and Yorkshire.

The Right of Ferae Naturae

The right to hunt the wild animals of the common: hares, rabbits, muntjac. Commoners negotiated limits and took stock of species.

Gleaning

The widely practised custom of walking the fields after harvest and picking up the stray barley, turnips. A bit like skipping in supermarket bins.

because with private property came a new concept, absolute dominion, which included the right to extract, exploit and even destroy anything on land that you owned.

Over a period of several centuries, the English countryside was irrevocably changed: it was emptied of commoners, who entered the cities to become faceless 'labour'; the collective decision-making, the sustainability and reciprocity of commons culture was replaced by the whim of individual landowners, and the countryside was left unprotected against a profit-driven management of nature. The diversity of English commons culture, its inclusivity, was replaced by the cold rationale of total dominion. As a result, over the last thousand years, the only voices that have been heard in the English countryside have been those belonging to white male landowners of extreme wealth. They have been the decision-makers and the profiteers, and their peccadillos and biases have reshaped the countryside and defined our nation. But they are not the only voices of England.

THE ENCLOSURE OF IDENTITY

The Countryside Alliance (CA) was set up in response to Tony Blair's proposed free vote on the banning of hunting with hounds. They gathered first in 1997, and their marches grew until some 400,000 people came together in 2002 for the Liberty and Livelihood march, which was at that point the largest protest in London's history. Alice Dunsdon, senior master of the Surrey Union Hunt, describes her experience of the first march on the CA website: 'The energy was spine tingling ... It was so brilliant because for the first time in history the entire countryside was united. Hunting, fishing, shooting, coursing, you name it, we were there.'

The *entire* countryside? The CA has 100,000 members and claims to represent the 11.4 million voices of rural inhabitants. But the organisation was set up as an amalgamation of the British Field Sports Society and the Countryside Business Group. Today, it describes itself as a 'campaigning organisation that promotes the rural way of life in parliament, in the media and on the ground'. But who, other than hunters and businessmen, gets to define what that rural way of life is?

There *should* be a countryside alliance, one that does exactly what the current one claims to do: 'give rural Britain a voice'. But it should be

CULTURAL EXCLUSION HAS A HUGE IMPACT. IT KILLS OFF CULTURE IT KILLS OFF TRADITION AND IT HURTS PEOPLE WHO WE COULD PROBABLY LEARN A LOT FROM.

Ruth Sullivan, Romany Traveller, from a speech made at the
Landscapes of Freedom Mass Trespass, 24 July 2021

a much broader church, and it should include voices that represent all of England's diverse communities. Perhaps more controversially, it should also represent urban voices, because wherever we live, and whoever we are, we all have a vested interest in our countryside. There is no actual line between the urban and the rural, there is no actual barbed-wire fence that prevents city dwellers from leaving the city. But there is a wall of semiotics built around the countryside that pretends city dwellers have no stake in it and no right to an opinion. There is a cultural hegemony that has been in control for so long that it pretends, and in some instances genuinely believes, it speaks for all of us who live there. It does not.

Our understanding of the English countryside, of England itself, has been privatised by those that own it. By imposing severe sanctions on the amount of England we are allowed to see for ourselves, England is increasingly being represented by private interests and becoming increasingly suspicious of those that do not conform to their vision of England – from the Gypsy, Roma and Traveller (GRT) community, to people of colour, to LGBTQ+ people.

Because they are marginalised from society, these communities are marginalised from the countryside too. Or perhaps it's the other way round. Both the symptom and cause of marginalisation are that these groups are rarely heard. So, in a bid to begin a wider, much more inclusive conversation about the countryside, for a better communal understanding of the various barriers that block people from nature, we asked members of six marginalised communities to express their personal experience of the countryside.

Sam Siva

Land worker

I was born in Montego Bay, Jamaica. I grew up in the hills, a rural setting. There was no rubbish collection, no internet and plenty of space for me to run wild.

I was seven when we moved to north-west London, and the contrast was huge. We did get out to the countryside sometimes, family trips to the seaside or the Lake District, but it was a different experience of the countryside to what I had grown up with. We weren't exploring, we were visiting; it was a very limited experience of nature. And even then, I still remember how my family were stared at. We stood out, we didn't feel welcome. That was part of our holidays.

I went through a period as a teenager where I became dismissive of the countryside. The city was exciting and there were more people there that looked like me. But when I went to university in Sussex I began to explore the countryside there. It had a huge effect on me. I was a very anxious student, very quiet, not at all like the loud child I used to be. I was overwhelmed by being around so many people that were different to me. There weren't many students of colour, not many people from the city, but slowly I started to make friends with people who had been brought up in the countryside, people who were used to taking long walks in nature. That made it less intimidating, being with people who knew what boots to wear and where to go.

Being a person of colour in the countryside, I have experienced a wide range of racism. From micro-aggressions and staring, to someone telling me

I look just like a golliwog, and saying the N-word – all these things make it harder to feel like you fit in. And they ruin the moment. I go to visit a friend, go into nature or to a country pub, and someone will say something. I can get over it, I've got my white friends and I feel supported by them, but it can still be a lonely feeling. In the city, if someone says something racist, I know there are other people around me who have also been racialised, who can empathise with me. But in the countryside, I'm left feeling like it is me who is making other people feel uncomfortable. Me being there has exposed this person as being shitty – to their friends, to the other people in the pub. It's different for different people, but for me, it's like I've internalised a psychosis, a trauma, that it's my fault that person said something nasty, that the atmosphere has turned nasty.

Recently, things seem to be improving. I spend lots of time in Wales, Dorset, Devon, the West Country, and I've felt fine. Maybe it's something personal, that I feel more confident because I have friends of colour who have grown up there and know the ropes. But I think the uprisings in the last couple of years have made the change more palpable. English people feel like they can't be racist, like it's an American thing, but their awareness is growing now; also, you're seeing a lot more people of colour in the countryside. Things are definitely changing.

Jim Ghedi

Folk singer

I only started to think about my background, or my class, in my late twenties. I was raised as a single child of a single mum, who moved around a fair bit for work. I've lived with grandparents on and off, and I've frequently had destructive male role models who suffered with addiction/alcoholism, unemployment and mental health problems.

It was only when getting into the music scene that I twigged that my experience was different. I'd go out on tour, come back and work three jobs to keep the rent up. Other people would come home and have the time and space to practise, record or find ways of relaxing and recouping. But if you're from a working-class background, your external realities are less secure, you're standing on less of a foundation. By and large, the jobs you work are temporary, low-skilled, low wage – hospitality, pulling pints in a pub. There's nothing in the way of a fallback.

But when it came to the countryside, I was really lucky. There's about eight miles of accessible green space around my home that incorporates working-class towns and villages situated in the South Sheffield region. Some of them are ex-mining communities, and some of the woods around there used to be the mines they worked in. People are connected to the countryside by history, but also because they use the space. Dog walking, kids hanging around with tinnies, cyclists, local wildlife and walking groups, lads fishing by the river, going up the top of the hill for a spliff before heading to the pub – people from working-class communities are always out in the open space wherever it's available. Even in inner-city Sheffield, around more urban spaces such as London Road, you can see kids congregating in the parks like they do in chicken shops or outside booze shops. We are all intrinsically attracted to these open spaces.

The thing is, the way the countryside is presented to us, you don't see those groups. Take a look at the Peak District National Park website, or the National Trust; you're not going to see kids in tracksuits and caps, but the same old middle-class image of a family on holiday. The countryside is all about tourism; it's a commodity. But what about the communities that actually live round there, who use it, who aren't just up on a weekend break? You don't see them because the image of the countryside that has been sold to us is clothed either in tweed or high-grade walking gear. The working class is seen to vulgarise the countryside – they look wrong or 'out of place'.

Around Sheffield, there is such a strong radical history of access rights and workers' movements, which has shaped the landscape we see today. However, there is dire need for further, wider and more accurate representation of working-class communities and their connections to the countryside. These communities need more ownership and rights to the land around them. Large areas are still owned by private landlords, who might provide a concession path if you're lucky, but there is an urgent need for local land rights and access paths to be distributed back to the community and made public, so they aren't lost in the years ahead.

There's a guy I see out and about who walks his two red setters every morning before work. He knows every name for every stretch of field and woodland round here. He knows local stories and folklore, things that have been passed down through generation after generation. He knows which paths hold the oldest tree species, where to find the bluebells in spring, where to find the lapwings every year, where the roe deer can be seen at sunrise, the buzzards, the kestrels, what each season's turning brings. He's just as valuable as a professor who studied landscape history. The people around here are very protective of the land, so when the fracking came, or new developments, or the felling of trees, they banded together, showed solidarity and resisted. They defend what they love.

Josie George

Writer and author of A Still Life: A Memoir

My mobility has been affected since I was a little girl. From about the age of eight, there were times where I couldn't walk without a great deal of pain from my waist down. This pain came coupled with a deep, chronic fatigue, where any exertion or activity could wipe me out for weeks. We used to say, in my family, it was like someone had pulled out my plug – that's how it felt. I just couldn't function any more. I spent more and more time off school. First they put it down to a post-viral illness or a neurological sensitivity, but to this day we still don't know what makes my body work differently.

When I did make it into school, little was done to accommodate my body. They just parked me out the way. During sports activities, I would sit on the sidelines reading my books, and since my high school had no wheelchair access, I spent a whole year in one room, having work brought to me. Friendships were hard because they rely so much on group participation – and I just couldn't join in. I think I was seen as a bit of a Debbie Downer, someone who would just make things less fun. This affected my own sense of self, my own idea of what made me fun.

There is a sense that people with disabilities must be depressed or joyless. But over the years, I've learned to carve out my own sense of fun, and my joy has seemed somehow rebellious and unexpected to people. My fun doesn't look much like other people's fun – I can't pretend to look cool. I need a lot of help to be out and about; I need a lot of accommodations, help from other people, a lot of tools to enable me. It can look awkward and weird to the

---

outside. Just going out into the rain the other day, I needed to wrap myself up in a big waterproof sleeping bag. My ears and eyes are sensitive, which means I have to wear special glasses and often ear protection. Temperature really affects the amount of pain my body feels – coldness means a lot of extra nerve pain in my face, so I'm all wrapped up to the nines, sat in my mobility scooter, ear muffs and all – that's not everyone's picture of cool, but I have a great time.

I don't get to be outside on my own very often. Independently I can get to my local graveyard on my scooter, or the old railway line near my house, which is now a paved greenway. Everywhere else I need to use a wheelchair, and that means a great deal of assistance and a whole lot of planning. To get out to Cannock Chase, for instance, I need to ask a carer if they have any free time, arrange transport, know where parking is, and plan the whole trip around the availability of disabled toilets. That's a big one – I can't just go piss in a bush like everyone else, so I need to plan.

I think one of the aspects of nature that people enjoy is autonomy. They like to choose where to go, to follow their noses, to be led by their own curiosity. I never get that sense of freedom. I have to ask to stop and pause so I can take a picture, and even the direction I'm looking in is not something I get to choose. In some ways, that's become its own gift, because I get to really study what's in front of me, the granular detail of nature. But my wheelchair and mobility scooter are very limited in terms of where they can go. Most rights of way are out of the question, as I can't fit through the kissing gates. Any kind of variation in the path, roots on the ground, uneven ground, makes it virtually impassable for me. Plus, slopes: you never feel heavier than when someone is behind you, panting heavily, trying to push you up a hill. I end up going: I'm sorry, I'm so sorry. It's hard not to feel a lot of guilt and shame, like I should just have stayed at home.

My experience of the outdoors is always tethered in some way to humanity. That's both in terms of social infrastructure, but also personal relationships: you need a certain kind of relationship to keep asking for help and that vulnerability is difficult. It is harder because I think able-bodied people have a very specific view of what nature is and what we should do in it. The things that I value are space, light, autonomy and the freedom to move – but I'm not just looking for a bucolic scene to gaze at, I want full-on sensory experiences, the ability to get close to things, to build my own relationships and take my time. So much of our experience of nature, disabled or not, seems like society is saying: here is your little ready-meal nature experience, one size fits all. We are not allowed to be truly ourselves in nature, especially if we're different; we're expected to play a role. But we should all be allowed to have a natural experience that fits who we are, not one that fits us into a box. I want to be able to be my diverse, wonderful self, not packaged up and told to look out from the sidelines. If anywhere should welcome diversity, it's nature.

So, what do we need? First off, it's very hard to know in England what places are accessible for disabled people. There isn't really a resource that I've come across that tells you explicitly what amenities are on offer in natural spaces and what to expect in terms of accessibility. Second, infrastructure – those wooden walkways installed by councils or the National Trust, I love those. They've got me to places I never thought I'd get to. Some people may not like modifying nature for accessibility, but people forget, if you make paths that are suitable for wheelchairs, you also make them suitable for pushchairs, not to mention the elderly. And we're all going to get old.

But it's not just about changing the landscape, it's about changing the support we get to be independent. Access to nature sits on a well-being spectrum, within a much bigger picture of disabled people not getting the care and support we need. I can't even get into my local leisure centre, so I'm hardly going to get to go wild swimming.

It is hard not to sense the pervasive social feeling that we're a pain, that to accommodate our needs is somehow undesirable, that it's a really heavy thing. The things that we need come parcelled with the feeling that we've spoiled it for able-bodied people – spoiled the picture, spoiled the experience. But nature is all about adaptation, and I feel like I fit into that picture, with all my tools, machines and ear mufflers. If we're going to increase access to nature, we need to grow a community around it that supports people in being who they are. There needs to be a change in society that helps us take care of each other.

Ruth Sullivan

Young carers manager

I only discovered my Romany heritage as a teenager. My mum had spent
her whole life without knowing, until one day my grandad just told her. She
thought he was joking. But he was getting older, he was quite sick, and sat
round the fire one night, he just had this 'fuck it' moment and told her.

He had fallen in love with a gorger (a non-traveller), and her family were
dead against the match. So he had this choice: whether to keep quiet about
his heritage and marry the woman he loved or not. My nan, his wife, also
had to stand up, at a time when women really weren't expected to state
their mind, and stick by him, because that's what she wanted. They both
had to make compromises, but the issue of him being a Gypsy was the real
problem. He was a cobbler by trade, and was, I suspect, also alert to the fact
that people wouldn't use his trade so much if they knew his origin. So he just
kept quiet for his whole life.

When my mum heard about her heritage, she just came out with it to me.
She was a single mum and didn't have another adult to process it. I think
she just sat with it, but for me, I wanted to unpick it, make sense of it. I'd had
quite an itinerant childhood anyway; because my dad was in the air force,
we grew up moving from base to base, always in these tight-knit closed
communities, always on the outskirts of society, but somehow more accepted
than travellers. I realised I felt proud to be Romany.

I never got to speak to my grandad about it and there was nobody left that
I knew of his generation to talk to. But I began to research my family history

and re-engage with the community. They were warm and welcoming, and from the off it felt real and right to me; there's something quite innate when you find people of your own culture, these people make sense to you. Relearning your own culture's language, like a child, is a weird experience.

I was a teacher, so speaking in public was never really a problem, and I've been using that to support the GRT community. I feel like I'm undoing some of the stuff that happened to my grandad, and speaking to Romany people, I feel like I'm getting closer to him. But afterwards, people still come up to me and feel entitled to say, 'You're not one of the bad Gypsies. You don't steal, you pay your taxes, you're OK.' They say whatever they like to your face; they don't mean you. I don't want to be the acceptable face of Gypsy culture. You accept me, you accept us all.

I really don't understand the bigotry, the ability for everything else that someone has achieved to be forgotten under the word 'Gypsy'. It's the acceptable bigotry; people in society feel able to say stuff about travellers that they wouldn't dream of saying to people of colour. It's always been of value to a given authority to demonise the travelling way of life, because it runs so contrary to the idea of servitude, lordship and ownership, the idea that your labour belongs to someone else – that's what scares authority.

But now it's everywhere: from broadsheet papers to documentaries on TV. My local MP, Tim Loughton, has been dining out on the fact that he kicked some travellers out of the park, so I wrote to him on Twitter, and asked him: first, did you ever speak to any of the constituents who are travellers, and second, could you tell me how many spaces are available in local transit camps? And he blocked me. Or another example, during GRT History Month, the *Argus*, Brighton's local paper, posted articles about travellers being where they shouldn't be. This article had a hundred-odd comments calling for imprisonment or death, inciting racial hatred in a way they couldn't with any other community. When you ask them for evidence, they say, 'Well, if you google it, you get loads of articles about travellers leaving a mess.' But of course you do, that's all they ever write about.

In terms of the police, Romany people are disproportionately targeted; we're more likely to be stopped and searched and more likely to get custodial sentences. By standing up and being Gypsy, you put this target on yourself. But with Priti Patel's policing bill, there is a general feeling that we're on the brink of losing our culture entirely, that this is an act of cultural genocide. What's happening is enforced assimilation: even though most of us don't live on the road, the right to travel is part of who we are. If we were a nomadic community in another country, people would support us, but there's a complete disinterest. If people aren't allowed to practise their culture, it just disappears in a matter of a few generations. And it affects us all; there's a lot of gorgers who don't fit in, who don't want to be worker ants and assimilate into the system. But if you stand by and allow this bill to go forward, it's a race to the bottom. If you let it happen to one group of people, you're giving permission to the state to tell you where you can live, what language you can speak, what kind of person you should be.

James Aldridge

Artist, queerriver.com

When it comes to talking about queer people and green spaces, the emphasis often falls on the subject of gay men and sex ('where there's greenery, there's queenery'), but this stereotype fails to consider other members of the wider LGBTQ+ community, or indeed the whole queer person – who they are when they are not having sex, which for most of us is most of the time. For me, queerness is more about how you relate to society in general, how you fit in with mainstream culture. And if you don't fit in, it's because someone somewhere has decided what or who you should be; more often than not, this person is in power: they have the money, they own the land.

I grew up in Hitchin in Hertfordshire, which is a market town small enough that you can walk into the countryside from town, which is how I seem to measure places. I always knew I fancied men, but as a child, being gay simply didn't seem like a possibility. Because I couldn't see myself reflected anywhere, I grew up with a distinct lack of self-awareness, not knowing there was an option to be queer. On television, growing up in the seventies and eighties, there was just this John Inman-style caricature of camp, and then in society, there was Thatcher's Section 28, which forbade the promotion of homosexuality, banned queer books, music and films, and presented queerness as evil. I couldn't see myself in any of it. Even today in the countryside, it can sometimes feel like my husband, my son and I have to come out again and again as a queer family.

Growing up, my favourite times were spent in the garden, drawing or watching woodlice have babies, or walking in the woods or by the sea. Growing older, I went to a very traditional boys' school – a comprehensive that seemed to think it was Eton or Rugby. The atmosphere was very gruff and macho, and didn't give me the space I needed to be me. When I was outside walking or playing, I was surrounded by the more-than-human and could feel like I belonged. I feel like we had a lot more freedom when I was a child than many children do now, paddling in the local brook, riding my bike and climbing trees. I was always looking around for things that I could collect – stones, fossils, feathers – and I began to build my own personal museum in my bedroom. I guess I was doing then what I do now for a living.

Not long ago, as part of my Queer River research project, I wanted to walk the length of the Salisbury Avon, the river nearest my home. But it didn't take me long to realise that I wouldn't get very far without trespassing on private property. That put me off instantly. I'm not comfortable with any confrontation, and that feeling of anxiety that it could happen anytime along the way completely put me off. Instead, the walks became more about meeting places and crossing points, little glimpses of the river as it met public footpaths and bridges. Trespass as most people understand it just isn't an option for me, as it carries the burden of feeling completely unsafe and of not belonging, when what I want from time in the countryside is a sense of connection.

I'm fascinated by what you could call the 'queerness' of rivers. For me, queerness is beyond just a concept of gay or straight; it's about how you respond to labels and boundaries imposed by society. Queerness is about being fully yourself, not changing yourself to fit existing systems and structures, whoever you happen to be. Rivers are just like that. To be healthy, rivers need to be allowed to overspill their banks, flood out beyond the margins. When you consider the water cycle or the water table, it's impossible to pinpoint where the river starts and ends, what its boundaries are. Queering is about blurring boundaries, and that's what rivers do so naturally, when they are allowed to.

The queerness of what we've come to call 'nature' inspires much of what I do. My work as an artist-educator is about taking a child-led and creative approach to learning, focusing on a child's ability to reach a state of 'flow' through playful and embodied engagement with the world of which they are a part. If we adults can encourage them to find where they fit, to experience their oneness and interconnectedness with their environment, following their instincts and learning through immersion in the landscape, then we can move away from the top-down approach of telling children and young people how or who to be.

We can all learn about ourselves – what we like, who we are, how we relate to the bigger picture of life – by immersing ourselves in natural systems. This allows us all to blur the boundaries between ourselves and the rest of nature, to experience ourselves as part of the integral nature of everything that is. It's healthy for us as individuals, and it's what the wider world needs from us too.

Eve Carnall

Author of Pollinating Change: The Buzz Tour

I walked 1,500 miles across England for five months, dressed as a bee, wild camping as I went and living off whatever I was given. I called it the Buzz Tour. It was a way to gather ideas and share them. Sometimes people would walk with me and experience their own changes and be inspired. But for most of the five months I was alone. I wanted to find out why some people were doing things about climate change, and why others weren't; I wanted to get to know my country and its people better, and record a slice of history. I had read a walking book from the seventies and was shocked at how much habitat had been lost and how much society had changed, how much my idea of 'normal' was different.

So I zig-zagged back and forth up the country, from Totnes to Berwick-upon-Tweed, doing between ten and fifteen miles a day and committing myself to observing as much as I could. I'd write down everything I noticed and visit environmental projects and passionate people and interview them. Every village had someone; everywhere I went people cared and were doing things, often with no online presence, and usually they didn't know about each other. They often felt so alone, not knowing others who cared enough to act were just a short walk away. It was such a blessing to find them and hear their stories. I had whatever money and food I was given, I slept in a room if it was offered, or I slept out. I almost never had to ask for anything other than water. People were curious and wanted to help. I could bring people gifts that others had given me, listen to stories, give words of encouragement, or pass on the stories of others to give them hope. Sometimes I would arrive in just the right place at just the right time to make a difference.

That journey was the most vulnerable and dependent that I've ever been. Every day felt like falling forward and being caught again by the kindness of others. I came to have a deep knowing that the universe connects people and I should trust it, but it was hard to do. I thought at the start I would get over the fear of wild camping as a woman alone, but I never did. It never got easier to sleep alone. When people would join me on the walk and camp with me, I felt so safe that I slept like the dead. There were several weeks where two female friends were with me and I felt so totally at home and in my habitat. It was a strange feeling. I hadn't felt at home on my own, but with them, every place we were was home.

Whether you're in the countryside or a city, there's a background noise of risk. It's not what happens, it's what you always know can happen, so there's a part of you on guard. One more amusing aspect was that pretty much every time I, a woman walker with a large rucksack, walked into a pub, the barman and customers would be waiting for my boyfriend to come in after me. They apologised sometimes, but I'd just laugh and say it happens all the time. I was cautious around pubs in general; I've found drunk men can switch quickly from compliments to threats. I'd never

discuss where I would camp in a pub, and when leaving I'd make sure no one could see where I went. One time in a pub, a group of men came up to me, asked me what I was up to, but the conversation turned dark as they questioned me in disbelief, saying they'd never let their girlfriend do something like that. They were fascinated, asking questions about my safety, what weapons I had brought with me (deliberately none), then telling me lengthy stories about local murders and rapes, saying that what I was doing was not wise at all. I think there's a societal pressure on women not to take risks, that you're being reckless, that if something happens to you, you brought it on yourself.

The further I got away from cities, generally the safer I felt. Looking for a place to camp, I would try to read both the natural environment and the human environment to find the safest places. I felt safer the further I was from a car park (most people don't walk very far from their car), somewhere with no empty booze cans or litter (because that would indicate partying or people who didn't care about others or their surroundings). In the morning, camping on private land, I'd get up early to avoid being seen and having any confrontations with landowners, but that was easy, because the fear meant I woke very easily, at the slightest of sounds, with fractured sleep.

I came to accept that fear was part of the price I had to pay to go on this trip. I would have liked to have done without it – I'd have got more sleep, had more energy – but I began to learn that part of my safety lay in my openness, my kindness and my friendliness. Being unthreatening, and not acting afraid, was a shield. Also, when people see you're trying to make things better, they're often compelled to help.

Because I was vulnerable and in need, people connected with me very quickly, and because I was passing through it was then or never. They'd just met me, but they would show me deep things about their lives and often invite me into their home. They were often very grateful someone else cared and was interested in what they were doing. And what I found was so hopeful. Everyone's perception of this world is this thin slice of reality, but the sliver I got, walking through England, was one of hope and creativity and inspiration, that you can't move without finding environmentalists. So many people care about our world, about the environment and the people around them. The lens of the media, that of a particular demographic of journalists, is not a true life experience. And the way that news is created – this one-way delivery system of bad news with barely any emotional response – is such an unnatural means of communication. That lack of emotion engineers apathy. It was a very different experience to get my news from people.

A few people were weirdly threatened by the Buzz Tour. It was as if their happiness and psychological wellness rested on the belief that there was nothing they could do. They needed me to be wrong, and would argue determinedly that I should give up. I think it was because if I was right, and there really are things we can do, then they might have to question why they weren't doing anything. I learned to recognise a 'vampire' and not to let those conversations go on long, to save my energy for people who needed it to keep them going. I know that hope takes practice, but you can look at any situation and choose to hope. The reality of the situation is out of my control, but how I look at it is not. Hope is the only possibility of a better outcome.

It's the same with being a woman in society. The background noise of threat is there, and it's my choice how to respond to it. I found by focusing on the positive, the goodness in people, you're more likely to bring it out of them. And that by standing up and being seen to act, people will join you.

MODERN ENCLOSURE

Enclosure is often misconceived as an historic trend. When the idea was first imported into the English countryside by William the Conqueror, it came on horseback, dressed in chainmail, wielding spears and swords. By Tudor times, it had donned the wigs of lawyers and the ermine robes of state, but still carried a sword behind its back to deal with the naysayers. And by the Georgian era, it wore the silken stockings of a squire and had discarded the sword in favour of a hangman's noose and a notice of arrest from the county court. These days it wears the pinstripes of land agents and corporate lawyers, and on weekends it favours the burgundy corduroy and blue-checked woollen shirt of the aristocracy in their dotage. But it is as alive today as it ever has been.

Once confined to the countryside, defended by gamekeepers carrying cudgels, it has now moved mainly to the cities, in the form of privately owned public spaces (POPS), sometimes called pseudo-public spaces. These usually appear in the form of plazas, atriums and small parks maintained by private developers, who are given carte blanche to decide who is allowed on them and what constitutes 'acceptable behaviour'. POPS are a new form

of privatisation of common space that works without the barbed wire; in its place are private security guards, dressed up to look like the police, whose job is to escort you out of this public arena the moment you do something their corporation disagrees with. They're not even obliged to publish the arbitrary rules that they've set. The premises are still public, but its premise is now private.

But during the lockdown year of 2020, enclosure experienced a resurgence in the countryside. Permissive paths were closed down, rights of way were chained off, private access to rivers was reinforced by newly erected razor wire and woodlands gained new CCTV and drone technology. Just after the first lockdown, the Ludlow Estate, owners of twenty square miles of the Dorset countryside, filed a petition to the government complaining that lockdown had brought a 'younger and more geographically and culturally diverse cohort' to a corner of their property portfolio, Durdle Door Beach. Likewise, in 2021, Kings College in Cambridge blocked off the whole of Grantchester Meadows, which had been a popular bathing spot for the last 500 years. The message from the college was unclear. They cited safety and concern for the riverbank, but also couldn't help referring to 'antisocial behaviour ... including drinking and drug taking' (as if university students are not known for recreational use of both).

Though no one acknowledged it directly, 2020 saw a massive influx into the countryside of 'the wrong sort of person' – in the eyes of those who own it – and with it came a rebarricading of the land.

On top of lockdown enclosure, there is a constant stream of neoliberal enclosure. New housing estates on greenbelt land, new industrial estates in forests, these enclose us from nature not necessarily by fencing it off, but by obliterating it altogether. The new HS2 train line has done both; it has destroyed areas of ancient woodland, but also cut what remains in half, segregating one side from the other. Similarly, just as the first lockdown began, signs went up around Weekley Hall Wood, near Kettering in Northamptonshire, informing the public that the wood was about to be fenced off and razed to the ground to make way for five new warehouses. In spite of over seven hundred people using the woodland on weekdays and upwards of a thousand at weekends, in spite of the mental and physical health benefits it brings to its community, the Duke of Buccleuch is entitled to eliminate this community resource simply because he owns the land. This, like HS2, is enclosure by obliteration.

TAKE ACTION FOR ACCESS

If you notice a modern enclosure, research the history of the place, what led to its privatisation and the context of the new barrier.

Gather some friends and trespass it.

Publish your trespass at TrespassersCompanion.org.

If the modern enclosure concerns a right of way, report this to the Ramblers (search for their app or online platform called Pathwatch).

RECLAIMING OUR COMMONS CULTURE

Enclosure took away our right to access English nature. It directly contributed to our current crisis of nature-deficit disorder, to our mental health problems due to our sedentary culture, and to the entrapment of the working class and their labour. But there is another, lesser-told story: when the fences went up around England, commoners lost not only their rights to the wealth of the land but also their ability to play with it, to create with it and to be inspired by the land – to collaborate with nature. They lost their culture. And as a result, we modern commoners were born without ours.

Over hundreds of years before enclosure, there were thriving, localised customs that were shared among districts – strands of craft, talent and skill that wove together to form tradition. English folk music represents just one strand of this culture that remains today, one fruiting body from the roots of English commons culture. But just as hip-hop has its four pillars – turntablism, MCing, breakdancing and graffiti – so English folk culture was more than just song and dance.

These days, most of us don't need estovers, turbary or piscary. We rely on radiators to heat our homes; we buy our food from the supermarket. But with the passing of these formalised customs came the forgetting of our traditional arts. The Heritage Crafts Association, an advocacy group for traditional heritage crafts, has put fifty-six of these crafts on their critically endangered list, including oak bark-tanning and currach-making. What is striking is how many crafts there once were, the wide variety of skills people developed while working with nature.

Another way to regain our 'commons culture' is to step into the land once again and gather the materials we need to resurrect the old arts. Commons culture is informed by history, but is in constant evolution; it has orthodoxies, norms and best practice, but it is determined by no overarching template, no centralised rule-maker. You can make of it what you want, because it is yours already. It is inclusive, it welcomes all who engage with it, and the only criteria for membership is participation – and respect for the land.

Here are just a few examples of the old crafts and traditions that have almost been extinguished from our culture, just as we were evicted from our land. Getting stuck into one or more of these crafts begins to change the way we relate to the land; it gives our walks a new purpose and sharpens our eyes to otherwise overlooked features of the landscape. But it also allows us to understand the flora of our land in a more visceral way, to understand it as a material, to test its strength and pliability, to learn with our hands. And it imbues us with a deeper understanding of the societies, not just English, that once lived close to nature – their customs, their ideologies, how they related to the world outside.

Stick-Making

Let's start with the finest country art: stick-making. On the surface, stick-making is nothing at all; it is nature who makes the stick after all, and all commoners have to do is find it and cut it. But look a little closer at the sticks on sale at country fairs or in local country post offices, and you'll find that the true art of stick-making is in the refinery – the careful, detailed handiwork that takes an ordinary object and turns it into a true collaboration between the human and non-human.

First, pick the stick. Go in winter, when the sap is at its lowest ebb. Take a walk in the woods or along the hedgerows and look for a length of stick that is straight enough and long enough to be of use. The crucial element here is to look at how the stick joins to the thicker branch, because this join is often used to create its handle. You might want to carve a smooth knob for the handle, or forge some kind of decorative feature, or you might want to look for a Y-shaped thumb stick (a switch that splits at its top, so you can rest your thumb in it). Whether you want a walking stick, a wizard's staff, a shepherd's crook, a crutch or something more ornamental is entirely up to you and how you cut it.

Hazel is perhaps the most common wood for sticks, largely because it is light to carry and often forms those convenient Y-shaped forks. Holly was writer Roger Deakin's favourite wood for sticks, and often grows arrow straight, thirsting for light. But by far the best wood for stick-making is blackthorn, once favoured by witches for their wands, and by the Irish for shillelaghs, a stout shaft of wood with a rounded, heavy end, a perfect tool for repelling the colonialist advances of the English. When weapons were banned by the English army in Ireland, shillelaghs were carried as walking sticks that could double as skull-crackers, and a whole martial art developed in the practice of wielding them.

Once you have found a likely candidate, cut the stick with inches to spare on either side and take it home. Make sure your cut is diagonal, so that the remaining branch does not form a level platform for rainwater to pool and rot the wood below – this will ensure you haven't damaged the plant, that it has the capacity to regrow. You'll now have to let it season for a year, which means that your very first stick will take bloody ages. But eventually, you can get into a satisfying rolling seasonal motion, where winter is spent searching for sticks and cutting them, and the spring and summer are spent outside, turning last year's branches into walking sticks.

When the stick is seasoned,

dried of its sap, it is ready to bend. The true art of the walking stick is in its snooker-cue straightness, the manipulation of wonky nature to the straight line of human intervention. Look down the shaft of it like you're aiming a rifle, and see where its crooks and bends are. Then dip some old rags in water, dampen the crooked area, and if you're a seventeenth-century shepherd, place it on the hot embers of your pastoral mountain-top campfire to steam. For all those who don't wear a smock to work, many stick-makers use a heat gun for a few minutes over the area, pointing its column of hot air at the crooked spot. You can also place the stick over a boiling pan of water, with a tea-towel draped over the top. Then take the stick in your hands, place the crooked spot at your knee and bend the stick to shape. What you are trying to do is to raise the temperature of the wood so that its molecules loosen their bonds, allowing you to rearrange their structure. What you're trying to avoid is burning the bark.

The next step focuses on the top and the bottom of the stick. Many stick-makers like to cap their sticks with a metal cap called a ferrule, which usually involves carving off a rim at the base of the stick, sliding on the cap and hammering small dents into it so that it holds. Ferrules can also be spiky, so the stick stands

on its own when stuck into mud, or rubber, and can be used on tarmac and pavement.

The head is by far the most creative element to the stick. Some like to carve handles, either into sweeping crooks or into fox heads or quail silhouettes; some like to simply smooth off the original structure of the join, to follow the growth and highlight the grain of the wood. Some like to cut the raw handle off and add another element, such as the horns from a roe deer or a ram, soaked and straightened in a vice for months.

Stick-making gets you out into the woods and hedgerows, looking at the world in an entirely new way. Your head curls and curves under the trees, as if following a squirrel's path, looking for the branches, looking for the length and where the handle might be. But it's also a great way of showing landowners and farmers a purpose to your walk. The landowning community go weak at the knees for a finely crafted stick, and will more than likely drop their defences if you share something in common.

One step further: why not go and ask the farmers if they wouldn't mind you cutting a few staves. Tell them what you're looking for – for example, blackthorn, hazel or ash – and ask them when they're cutting the hedges (offcuts can make for very good sticks). Farmers and landowners are often amenable to people having tangible reasons for being on their land, especially if there is a finely crafted stick in it for them. Seeking 'permissive access' is a great first step to eliminating the barrier between farmer and rambler, allowing each to see the human behind the caricature.

Corn Dollies

Corn dollies come in all shapes and sizes, and were traditionally fashioned from the last leaf of whatever crop had been harvested – wheat, barley, maize and so on. Found all over Europe, the craft's roots are in pagan traditions, where the final sheaf of corn would be taken home and given to the oldest woman in the village, who would save it until next spring, when the seeds were sown for the next crop. The dolly would be dug into the ploughed earth, to bless the next crop with the success of the last. Sometimes the dolly would act as a rain charm and be doused in spring water before being put into storage.

There are a near-infinite number of different shapes to a corn dolly, each a localised expression of the tradition. Some would be shaped into bells, some into babies' rattles, and the few remaining in English folk museums carry the name of the town with them: the Cambridge Umbrella, the Durham Chandelier, the Suffolk Horseshoe, the Worcester

Crown, the Hereford Lantern and so on. Of course, when making yours, though you will undoubtedly learn lots by copying the masters, allow yourself to experiment and create your own designs. Folk culture is not about sticking to the rules; in fact, it positively encourages deviation.

A subset of the corn dolly is the countryman's favour, usually a woven plait of three straws tied into a loose knot to represent a heart. This has fewer ties with pagan custom; typically a young man would pick up a few straws after the harvest, arrange them and give them to the woman of his fancy. If she was wearing the favour next to her heart when he saw her again, then he would know that his love was reciprocated.

Ink-Making

Go out, get some nature, put it in a pan with some water, boil it down for several hours. That's about the sum of it. You can make ink out of pretty much any organic matter, and many plants and their roots have surprising colours when extracted. The aim of the simmering is to extract the natural colour, and the point of boiling is to concentrate the colour, to make it stronger. Make sure you remove the organic mulch before boiling, and if you like, you can blend it up to make paper. Once you've got your dark, sticky liquid at the bottom of the pan, you'll need to add cloves so it doesn't go mouldy, and add a solution of cherry sap or gum arabic, to keep the ink from flaking off the paper. When you've got a few inks, the real work begins. Experiment with solutions of iron oxide (chuck some nails in a jar with vinegar and water) to make it darker, or citric acid (lemon juice) to make it lighter. *Wild Colour* by Jenny Dean is a great way into natural ink-making.

Charcoal

Easy-peasy. Get some twigs, wrap them in foil, bung them in the fire, take them out, draw with them. Practice makes perfect. The best wood for charcoal is either spindle or willow.

Wild Clay

Digging clay was once a common right called marling. Back in the day, clay was the plastic of our modern age; you could use it to make pots and cups, crockery for the kitchen or large amphoras for storage, but it was also used as a substitute for cement. Cob houses were built of a mixture of clay, small stones and straw, and clay was also used as daub, to line and insulate the interior walls of houses.

Clay can be found and dug very easily. Check the maps provided by the British Geological Survey (bgs. ac.uk) for large clay deposits and go out into the land; ideally, look for tiny streams that run through the woods, meaning the water will have done most of the digging for you. Find thick wet deposits of the stuff, and trowel it into your bag. Once you have got your bag of soil and clay, you'll need to process it, to rid it of imperfections that will cause the pot to crack when it is fired.

First, put the clay in a bucket and begin stirring it. All that is clay will dissolve into the water, and all that isn't will sink to the bottom. Once you've created a greyish, custard-thick slip (a solution of clay and water), run it through a sieve four or five times, decanting the soil away from the solution. Pour the remaining slip into a pillowcase and leave it to drip-drain in the sun for a few days. What remains is your clay. Mould it into whatever you like, reshape the earth to your creative vision. You can then dig yourself an earth kiln and feed it wood for an entire day while it bakes, or, much easier, google the nearest pottery workshop or kiln in your area and go fire it there. You may be surprised at how many pottery firing services there are near you. If you're really serious, you could even invest in your own kiln. Though be warned: they don't come cheap.

Herbal Medicine

Nature is one big pharmacist's store cupboard. You might have to read some of the Italian-American theorist Silvia Federici's work to truly appreciate all the reasons why we have forgotten this, but the persecution of wise working-class women, together with the masculinisation of the medical profession, not to mention the enclosure of the commons, is about the sum of it. But though the patriarchy has forced us to collectively forget it, it won't stop every verge, meadow and woodland in England growing a whole host of medicines just waiting to ease your gripes, pains, snivels and sores.

To pick a few off the pack: comfrey is a great topical medicine for

arthritis, bruises, sprains and burns. 'Topical' means it must be applied to the specific area, and certainly not ingested; comfrey in particular can damage the liver if consumed. So great is the healing properties of yarrow that the great Greek warrior Achilles carried it with him into battle. Yarrow works well as a salve, poultice or balm to heal wounds, cuts, abrasions and burns, soothing pain and stimulating healing. The roots and leaves of burdock can be used to clear the skin of acne and eczema, and also, when ingested, can purify the liver. Finally, the most common weed in England, plantain, can be mashed into a pulp to soothe wasp stings.

There are a plethora of different, specific ways to apply these herbs to heal the body, and just as many different ways to preserve them. You can dry the leaves and roots, pestle them up and pour the powder into capsules, to be taken daily. You can create tinctures by soaking fresh or dried ground herbs in alcohol, which preserves them for at least a year, taking one, two or a few drops a day. You can make poultices, infused oils, balms and salves, and of course, easiest of all, you can make up a delicious cup of herbal tea. The healing properties of nature, and how to capture them, is a whole world in itself, and the best way in is through expert advice, reading, YouTube videos and social media.

TAKE ACTION FOR ACCESS

Check out the Heritage Crafts Association's website (heritagecrafts.org.uk) and see how you can get involved in keeping traditional craft skills alive.

Have a look through the HCA's redlist of endangered crafts (heritagecrafts.org.uk/redlist), see which most appeals to you, and give it a go.

'If we really want to get ahead
of the litter problem, we need
to foster a strong, emotional
connection with community and
nature. We need to foster love.'

DOM FERRIS,
FOUNDER OF TRASH FREE TRAILS

One of the most popular arguments against greater public access to the English countryside is also the most valid: the problem of litter. The argument seems almost irrefutable: people bring litter everywhere they go, and the more people who have access to more places, the more litter we will see in our countryside. Scenes of discarded camping equipment in the Peak District, scattered face masks on our streets and overflowing bins in city parks littered the papers during lockdown, and this was used as ammunition against those seeking greater public engagement with nature. The message came loud and clear: the public cannot be trusted; how can we expect to be granted greater access to nature if this is how we treat what we have already?

People get very angry about litter. Littering is seen as a moral failing, sociopathic, something that has more to do with a character flaw than social science. People want litterers punished and shamed, and it always seems to be someone else who does the littering. But look again at those photos of overflowing bins, and they illustrate the cataract of outrage that blocks our vision. That the bins are overflowing clearly demonstrates not public negligence but, very simply, that there are not enough bins.

Litter is a practical problem, a systemic failure, and it will be solved by improved infrastructure, messaging and policy, not moral outrage. The sooner we stop clinging on to this idea of a moral failing, the better for nature. And like it or lump it, it falls to those campaigning for greater access to the countryside to figure out the litter problem. As ever, don't get angry, get organised.

THE STATE OF THE NATION

Let's get one thing out of the way. Picking up litter does not solve the larger problem with litter itself. On a global scale, picking up litter from the forest floor and transporting it to a bin does not help the earth. The difference between litter discarded or litter disposed of is simply one of location, depth and, sometimes, nation. When you, good citizen, have found and transported a crisp packet from the hedgerow to the bin, it will then be shipped off to a council depot, where it will then either be sent to a burial site or incinerator in England, or more likely, carted off on a big stinking ship to Malaysia or Turkey, where it will likewise be buried or burned. Out of sight, out of mind, but its toxicity is still very much in the earth's ecosystem. Whether your crisp packet exists for 500 years on the ground or beneath it, or is otherwise burned into the air makes very little difference to nature. Picking up litter is less a question of ecology than aesthetics. In other words, the problem with litter is not the littering, but the litter itself.

HERE ARE SOME OF THE BASIC FACTS ABOUT LITTER:

In 2016, the UK generated 222.9 million tonnes of waste, with England responsible for 85 per cent of it.

Construction and demolition is responsible for about a third of this waste, and the most littered item is fast-food packaging, but smoking also contributes dramatically to the problem – an estimated 4.5 trillion cigarette butts are dropped on this earth every year.

People on the move are more likely to litter. Motorists (53 per cent) and pedestrians (23 per cent) litter the most.

Roughly two-thirds of plastic waste in the UK is sent overseas to be recycled – in part, to reduce costs.

The Environmental Protection Act 1990 makes certain duty bodies legally responsible for keeping land that is under their control and to which the public has access clear of litter and refuse, and for keeping their highways clean, as far as is practicable.

If litter is dropped on privately owned land, it is either the owner or occupier who is held responsible for clearing this litter away.

Litter leads to litter: people litter more in areas already strewn with rubbish. But the same is true in reverse: less litter leads to people littering less. Which might be our way out of the problem.

POSITIVE TRACE

Leave nothing but footprints, take nothing but photos. This is the mantra of the 'Leave No Trace' ethic, an approach to being in the countryside with minimal impact. It is the result of a successful American campaign that began in the late sixties. Advances in technology for outdoor goods, lighter camping stoves, synthetic tents and more compact roll mats encouraged many more people out into the trails of America, creating an upsurge in litter. The response came from three bodies: the Forest Service, the National Park Service and the Bureau of Land Management, who were informed by a field of study called recreation ecology. This branch of social science assessed visitor impact on natural spaces and their relationship to influential factors, which culminated in a pamphlet they produced in 1987, titled 'Leave No Trace Land Ethics'.

The research hinged around the importance of communication – how best to influence people's actions. There were many trials and several errors: in one instance, an Arizona national park was having problems with people removing keepsake chunks of stone from an ancient petrified forest, so they put up signs about it. Unfortunately, recreation ecology found that on reading about how many people had stolen from the site, people were in fact encouraged to do the same. The signs caused an increase in theft.

But for all its good intentions, 'Leave No Trace' simply hasn't worked.

While it may persuade people not to add to the litter, it does not solve the issue of the litter already dropped. Any future advance of access rights in England will have to take on the mantra of Lawyers for Nature, an organisation that campaigns to give legal standing to trees and rivers, and propose a more dynamic theory of change: *Positive Trace*. Instead of asking people to be like ghosts on the land, to pass through unnoticed, they suggest a more dynamic, immersive and inclusive impact on the land: improving it. The Positive Trace philosophy asks people to take out bags with them, to collect the litter they find, to leave the land in a better state than had they not been there. Not only does this ethic actively clear the countryside of waste, but by asking more of people, you are inviting them to forge a deeper, more personal bond of care with the landscape.

TRASH FREE TRAILS

Glastonbury Festival is one of the biggest events in the countryside litter calendar. Every year that it is held, right-wing newspapers salivate at the opportunity to berate its snowflake clientele for their eco-hypocrisy. Because every year, these eco-posers leave behind a battleground of discarded waste, from tents to inflatable sofas, from tinnies to fag butts. In July 2019, the *Daily Mail* (never knowingly under-outraged) published a headline that sacrificed pithiness for indignation: 'What stinking hypocrisy! They cheered David Attenborough like a god at Glastonbury, but as the crowds headed home, they left a squalid mess that makes a mockery of their eco-posturing.'

Sadly, and typically, the *Mail* had embedded an undercover journalist deep in the Glastonbury compound, and when she awoke on Sunday morning, she was, sadly and typically, disgusted with what she found:

> **It is utterly disgusting, but sadly typical. The sight of field after field covered in rubbish has become the inevitable fall-out of the summer festival culture as people (usually young people aged 17–24) let their hair down, party their socks off and then stagger back to their middle-class homes leaving environmental carnage behind.**

But what the *Mail* failed to acknowledge is that every year the thousands of tonnes of litter left by revellers is picked up by over a thousand volunteers, who are also revellers. In return for free entry, the litter-pickers dedicate time

Artist's impression of a Daily Mail *journalist, undercover at Glastonbury*

during and after the festival to make sure the litter is cleared from the land – down to the last cigarette butt. The festival leaves no trace because people volunteer their time; they get the benefit of the festival because they have dedicated their efforts to making it sustainable. Michael Eavis doesn't farm knee-deep in plastic every year because he has created a *commons of care* – people get their rights because other people dedicate their responsibility towards the resource.

This model could be rolled out of Glastonbury into the rest of our nation. Though it won't satisfy the outrage of tabloid journalists, it might just solve the litter problem in the English countryside. Perhaps if attention was turned from castigating the few who leave litter to supporting the many volunteer groups who pick it up, we might come somewhere near to solving the problem.

Of course, there are already groups who are doing this, and doing it with great success. Trash Free Trails is an offshoot of the better-known Surfers Against Sewage, an NGO with an impressive track record of not only cleaning the oceans and rivers, but through doing so, sending the message that they shouldn't be polluted in the first place. Trash Free Trails has migrated this ethic onto land, bringing a flair for marketing, social media and business ethics to caring for the countryside that beats anything the government has initiated. In their own words, their mission is 'to reduce single-use pollution (aka litter!) on our trails and wild places by 75% by 2025 and (re)connect people with nature through purposeful adventure'.

At its most basic level, Trash Free Trails asks people to come together in their spare time and collect litter. They provide the infrastructure, the kit and the practical assistance, but they also frame the act of picking litter in a way that encourages people to do it. In their own words: 'Through an interconnected series of empowering and impactful community-led initiatives, we will activate a volunteer army of riders, runners, and roamers of all ages, who are ready and able to donate their time, passion and talent to the protection and promotion of their wild places.'

Trash Free Trails are masters of the rebrand. They have tinkered with the semiotics of litter picking, reframing it from a servile, low-status activity to something heroic. Their volunteers are called the A-Team, subverting the image of litter pickers as disgruntled retirees in anoraks and reframing them with the image of B. A. Baracus firing a machine gun from a van at 90 miles per hour. 'Purposeful Adventure' is their version of the Positive Trace ethic from Lawyers for Nature. By asking people to take a more participatory role in caring for the countryside, they demonstrate how rights and responsibilities can entwine towards a better environment. With just a twist on how it is presented, caretaking turns into stewardship – Trash Free Trails are investing litter picking with social capital.

Among their various schemes and activities, their Trash Mob Academy stands out as a way of effecting change in the present and the future at the same time. The Trash Mob Academy takes schoolchildren out on adventures into the countryside, picking litter as they go, and teaching them about impact: the repercussions of our actions on the ecology. Another scheme is Trail Bandit Bingo, where litter picking is reinvented as a game, something with reward value.

On top of all this, they are using their volunteer force to collect vital statistics on litter to provide the artillery for the attack on our systemic failures. The conclusions of their research are striking and paint a much more positive picture of the future than the outrage in the press. First of all, as already stated, there is a spiralling effect of a cleaner countryside – less litter in a place leads to less litter. Second, the act of picking up litter doesn't just benefit the environment, but also the community that comes together to clean – picking up litter has been shown to improve the mental health and sense of community cohesiveness among the volunteers. And third, on a much wider level, a regular connection to nature has been shown to make people more concerned about the wider environment, to change their behaviour in order to combat climate change.

This emphasis on community participation, on a deeper, more meaningful relationship with the outdoor world, a stewardship that has nothing to do with ownership but everything to do with belonging, is a modern expression of the old paradigm of the commons, promoting a return to traditional values with an up-to-date spin. The future is the past, with better infographics.

Currently, Trash Free Trails engages thousands of people who cover thousands of acres. Why not scale up their operations so they cover every inch of England? Why can't schemes like this be funded, why can't schools and universities be involved, why can't picking up litter be the way we teach the next generation about ecological impact, about the repercussions of our actions on natural habitats, and about our complicated relationship with nature?

Without focusing on litter picking, rather than litter dropping, no self-respecting campaigner for greater public access to the countryside can look a farmer in the eye and guarantee that there will be no increase in litter. Encouraging people not to leave litter is less pragmatic than facilitating people to pick it up, and because litter is by far the most cited reason against greater public access, actively resolving the problem opens the door to extending our rights of access. People earn access to the countryside by actively engaging with the health of its ecology. Sounds fair.

EXPERT WITNESS

Dom Ferris

*Founder and managing director
of Trash Free Trails*

I've got a real problem with the slogan 'Keep Britain Tidy'. 'Keep' implies that our countryside is already tidy. It isn't. Single-use plastic pollution, which is what we call litter, is increasing in the countryside, and that's got a lot to do with an ever-increasing level of production. Litter picking is a hamster wheel – we pick it up, more is produced, more is dropped, and we keep picking it up. It goes round and round. We live in a society that wants us to consume, and the other side of that is disposal – chuck it away so you can consume some more. There is a lack of acknowledgement for what the real causes of litter are. We're not going to pick our way out of the problem.

But the problem also has a lot to do with the way we react to litter. We are all too often outraged, as if outrage sorts the problem. We condemn the people that litter, but that just makes things worse: littering is a behaviour, and if you want to alter that behaviour, you need to give people the opportunity to change. Condemnation just freezes people in time.

I've always had anxiety and depression, and it really began to flare up about a decade ago. I was working for Surfers Against Sewage, organising their beach cleans, and the big moment for me was when I realised how much the beach cleans were doing not just for the beach but for me, internally. At the end of the day, with a beautiful clean beach, I felt proud of myself again; my day had purpose and meaning. Doing something good for the environment often has a sense of pious self-flagellation, like you're not allowed to enjoy it. Plastic pollution is a serious business, with serious effects, but it doesn't mean it can't be fun and fulfilling to tackle it.

The primary driver for me, if I'm really honest, isn't even about pollution and the environment – it's about empowering people to make a real difference, seeing first-hand the massive impact that happy, proud communities can have on the world. If you had to distil the issues we're facing environmentally, and with litter, into one word, it would be 'disconnection'. We are disconnected from our environment, from our communities and from ourselves. So our job at Trash Free Trails is to reconnect people to their environment and to their communities – and hopefully, to themselves – by giving them a sense of fulfilment. We do this through litter picking, but that's really just the activity that binds communities together; it's a means for people to learn about the environment, to tell new stories. The kids we're trying to connect with in the Trash Mob Academy are the very same kids the *Daily Mail* is blaming and shaming for littering. There's a whole machine out there to condemn them, but no one and nothing to show them the alternative. If we really want to get ahead of the litter problem, we need to foster a strong, emotional connection with community and nature. We need to foster love.

TAKE ACTION FOR ACCESS

Sign up to Trash Free Trails (trashfreetrails.org).

Create a group of litter pickers, work out an area to cover. This is your area, your commons, you are its commoners and the responsibility to keep it tidy is yours.

Meet up regularly to pick up litter, and when you do, tell people about it on social media using the hashtag #trespasslitterpick.

Get in touch with the landowners. Why not begin a dialogue: walk up to the farm door or estate office, and tell them of your intention.

An Essay on Canine Crapsack Proliferation (CCP)

Doggie-jobbies, trash-bag testicles, crapsacks – whatever you want to call them, if there is one issue that unites the various warring tribes of England, it is a deep disdain for the plague that besets our nation: Canine Crapsack Proliferation, or CCP. These filthy crapsacks are tossed into or (rather more creatively) hung from nature; like baubles decorating a crappy Christmas, they ornament our trees, hedges and footpaths, enraging everyone that sees them.

No one on earth likes dog crap. Apart from being generally disgusting, dog crap can spread diseases, including campylobacter, tapeworm, hookworm, roundworm, giardia and E. coli, and more rarely salmonella. These bacteria don't sit and fester where they fall, but instead their pathogens are leached into our groundwaters, our rivers and even up into our air. In America, bacteria from dog crap has been proven to cause regular algal blooms in the estuaries, which have caused beaches to be closed for swimming and shellfishing. A 2011 survey of air samples from Detroit, Cleveland and Ohio found that 10–50 per cent of the bacteria in the air came from dog crap lying on the ground. And back in England, the situation is worse than you might think. With an estimated 1,000 tonnes of crap being shat daily by Britain's 8 million dogs, this is an incremental excremental problem, and it's not going anywhere.

In the 1970s and 1980s, UK councils were deluged with complaints of a countryside besieged by dog crap, with a popular rumour that persists to this day that they were left so long where they lay, they turned white with age. As it happens, the phenomenon of white dog crap has more to do with the diet of dogs than any ageing processes. At the time, dog food consisted largely of bone meal. As a result, there was so much surplus calcium in dog crap that when it was gifted to pavement and country path, nature just had to wash off the surface matter, and its white, calcified skeleton remained.

The 1980s were a decade of discontent. But among the Falklands War and the Poll Tax riots, history has somehow forgotten the Middle England war of outrage, the high-tension, crappie-culture skirmish that was waged over dogs. In 1975, Thames Television screened an hour-long documentary entitled *The Case Against Dogs*, communicating the health dangers of dog fouling and the risk of toxocariasis, a warning that hitherto had been limited to the pages of medical journals. Toxocariasis is a rare disease caused by accidentally swallowing the microscopic eggs of the canine-borne worm *Toxocara canis*, which are dispersed in the faeces of infected dogs, causing – in some cases – blindness and asthma in humans.

However, with the scare came a counter-propaganda campaign launched by the hitherto unknown, but exceptionally well-financed, dog lobby. The charity PRO-Dogs, which brought together dog owners, breeders and vets in one united push, sought to challenge what it called this new, alarming wave of 'anti-dog hysteria'. They printed free pamphlets, established local branches for likeminded campaigners, and lobbied the government with marches and protests against the local authorities that had banned dogs from their parks.

Over the Atlantic, in New York, a similarly vicious battle was being fought, where dog crap had become an important milestone in the career of Mayor Ed Koch. He was responsible for setting into motion the first truly enforceable law demanding that dog owners pick up their pets' waste in the streets. The 'Pooper Scooper Law', as it became known, stated that 'a person who owns, possesses or controls a dog, cat or other animal shall not permit

Dogs are noble creatures, but they do produce a lot of crap

the animal to commit a nuisance on a sidewalk of any public place'. Again, this caused consternation among dog owners, who joined a campaign launched by the American Society for the Prevention of Cruelty to Animals complaining that this law would 'impose undue hardship on dog owners'.

Back in England, the issue looked set to divide the nation. It was not until 1996 that Britain finally introduced the Dogs (Fouling of Land) Act, a law that ushered in the modern regime of bins, signs, posters and prohibitive fines that placed responsibility on owners to remove dog waste from public spaces. Until then, for over a decade, the government was the perfect personification of prevarication: up crap creek without a paddle. Luckily, it being the 1980s, neoliberalism stepped into the place of government and devised a way not to solve the problem as such, but to monetise it. And so, the crapsack was born.

You can't polish a turd, but you can wrap it in plastic. Thus began a solution to the problem that made the problem much, much worse. What's worse for the environment than a tonne of dog crap? A tonne of dog crap gift-wrapped in plastic. But at the time, this seemed to be the golden bullet, the end of an argument, the solution to England's woes. Neoliberalism won the day: it has been fifty years since plastic crapsacks came onto the market, and today a search for dogshit bags on Amazon comes up with 3,000 results.

Just like plastic waste, dog crap is a booming industry.

More often than not, those confronted while in the act of CCP will retort with a paternalistic smile, saying, 'It's biodegradable.' More often than not, they're right, but this simply means that the bags will disintegrate into ever smaller particles of plastic, remaining there for anything from six months to a thousand years. Essentially, anything bar radioactive isotopes can be labelled as biodegradable, because most things will degrade over time. But this does not mean it stops harming the environment or that it eventually turns into organic matter. Essentially, in terms of crapsack proliferation, biodegradable is a meaningless term.

What CCPers *think* they are saying is that their dog bags are compostable, that it will be swallowed up by Mother Earth, no harm done. And their confusion is no accident. For years, the companies that produce plastic bags for CCP have been profiting from, and propagating, the confusion surrounding the terms 'biodegradable' and 'compostable'. A light was finally shone on this murky world in 2015, when the US Federal Trade Commission warned, in a letter to twenty crapsack manufacturers, that their products' environmental claims could be deceptive. Anything that purports to be biodegradable is supposed to 'completely break down into its natural components within one year', the letter stated. 'Most waste bags, however, end up in landfills where no plastic biodegrades in anywhere close to one year, if it biodegrades at all.'

But even if the bag is compostable, that doesn't mean it will compost while hanging at a jaunty angle from a hawthorn hedge. In fact, it is highly unlikely to do so. 'Compostable' refers to materials that have been certified to break down completely into non-toxic components (water, carbon dioxide and biomass) that will not harm the environment. But for many substances, including dog crap, this takes hot temperatures. Professor M. Leigh Ackland, a molecular biologist at Deakin University in Melbourne, Australia (who has been successfully composting her dog's crap for twenty-five years in her domestic garden compost heap) says, 'A high temperature is critical. With grass clippings it can reach 60°C (140°F). It has to be maintained, turned over, and not become too moist. But that temperature should kill most bacteria, including the toxoplasmosis found in poo.' And none of this applies to any of the crapsacks you find in nature.

By wrapping our dog crap in bags, what we're actually doing is preserving organic matter in an ecologically expensive plastic bag and sending it to a landfill, where it cannot decompose. And the scale of this problem is vast, because it is global. With 900 million dogs in the world, CCP is a significant ecological emergency. Governments and citizens have been scratching their heads to work out how to solve the problem and coming up with a diverse array of new solutions. Iran has recently banned dog walking, embracing dog crap into their pseudo-religious dogma, linking CCP to citizens 'blindly imitating Western culture'. In 2013 the mayor of Brunete, a small town twenty miles from Madrid, initiated a volunteer scheme to spy on fellow residents. Volunteers willingly tailed dog walkers, followed them on walks, collected the offending turds and brought them to a dedicated office with DNA-testing facilities. The shamefaced dogs were identified on the town's pet database, and the faeces were returned as lost property in a box bearing the town's insignia. The scheme was a success: the mayor reported a 70 per cent drop in CCP.

Taiwan made the same idea a lot more fun. Instead of recruiting a volunteer Stasi, they created a lottery. Residents in New Taipei city were offered a lottery ticket for every bag of crap they handed in. Officials collected 14,500 crapsacks from 4,000 people, with the scheme said to have halved the amount of excrement in the city and the winner of the lottery paid out in gold ingots.

Councils in England have tried a variety of different machines that efficiently suck up the waste without having to get their hands dirty. 'Poovers', as they are called, come in all shapes and sizes. In Hastings, there are wheelie bins with hoover nozzles; in Teesdale, they tried nifty Ghostbusters-style backpacks; Islington have merged poovers with motorbikes; and Nottingham council proudly use an all-terrain cart called FIDO (Faeces Intake Disposal Operation), which is capable of poovering up 240 litres of dog crap and converting it to slurry.

But there is one street lamp in the West Midlands that stands as a shining example to us all. By far the most ingenious solution to the problem of CCP has come from the mind of a retired engineer and amateur inventor Brian Harper. He has invented a generator that runs on the biogas produced by dog crap. Located on a popular right of way that leads through England's Malvern Hills, walkers can pick up a paper bag from a dispenser on the lamp, and when they return with the bag and its little brown gift, they can slot it into the lamp's biodigester. The microbes in the anaerobic digester produce methane, which is then stored and used to generate electricity to power the street lamp at dusk.

Brian Harper has said of his invention: 'I reckon that, conservatively, one in five dogs are having their poo picked up in plastic bags. Dog poo goes straight to landfill and becomes a major contributor to the methane gas

A shame-faced dog, crapping in nature

that comes out of landfill. But we grab the methane at source, and don't transport the waste or send it to an incinerator that gobbles up even more energy. And it's also a big reducer of the plastic-bag problem. I want to see this idea spread around the world and make a significant contribution to the reduction of greenhouse gases – as well as the problem of dog poo on our shoes.'

Brian is the best of us. He is a visionary who has sat down in his shed to solve a problem that has plagued us for half a century, and he has produced a workable, environmentally friendly source of power that has been used since neolithic times for fuel, but is also at the forefront of the new green wave of biogas solutions. In 2014, a company called GENeco launched its first Bio-Bus, the UK's first bus to be powered by gas generated from sewage and food waste. The bus (trialled *brilliantly* on Bristol's number 2 route) produces significantly less carbon dioxide than fossil fuels and runs for 300 kilometres before refuelling. The same company runs a sewage waste facility that injects enough electricity into the national grid to provide fuel for between 5,000 and 6,000 homes.

The answers are out there; they just need government backing and state finance and infrastructure to turn the tide of crap and clear up our country-side. However, but for one lone MP in 2015 – another visionary by the name of Anne Main – the halls of Westminster have been quiet on the subject. It is time for this to change.

BECOME A CRAPPPPPY CAMPAIGNER

In March 2015, Conservative MP Anne Main, representative for St Albans in Hertfordshire, stood up in parliament and demanded a 'Pragmatic Poo Strategy'. She stopped one short of passing a motion and ended her impassioned speech with these words:

Let me close with the poem that the
Forestry Commission likes everyone to read:

If your dog should do a plop, take a while and make a stop,
just find a stick and flick it wide into the undergrowth at the side.
If your dog should do a do, you don't want it on your shoe,
find a stick, pick a spot, flick into the bushes so it can rot.
If your dog should do a poo, this is what you should do,
just find a stick and flick it wide into the undergrowth at the side.
If your dog should make a mess there really is no need to stress.
Find a stick, pick a spot, flick into the bushes so it can rot.

With that, I rest my case, Mr Hollobone.

MPs were mystifyingly unmoved by Anne Main's efforts in parliament, and the notion of a comprehensive Pragmatic Poo Strategy dropped to the floor of the Commons, to be scooped up and binned by the Speaker. But we at Right to Roam refuse to let her legacy die. So we have launched the Campaign to Rid Albion of the Pestilence of Pooch Poo through Petitioning Politicians Yourself, or CRAPPPPPY. We call on you, the people of Great Britain, to write to your MPs, demanding an urgent Pragmatic Poo Strategy for your local area. A template letter can be found on trespasserscompanion.org.

TAKE ACTION FOR ACCESS

First, go to trespasserscompanion.org to download a template letter for your MP. Add your own experience, and add to the call for a Pragmatic Poo Strategy.

Second, when out walking, don't just spy a crapsack and let it lie. Take a photo, post it on social media, tagging the council and using the hashtag #endCCP and #doggydododontdo. Use the What Three Words app (what3words.com) to locate the crapsack within a metre-square accuracy, and tag the local council, asking them to clear it. This will either result in the crapsack being removed or add to a body of evidence.

Turd, tell your friends what you're doing. Sometimes you can only produce a movement by putting the effort in. Talk about CRAPPPPPY with your friends, persuade them to follow your lead, and write a letter to their MP.

'I think there is a serious disconnect between the practice and knowledge of science and average people: it's one thing to tell people about microplastics, but for them to see it for themselves is another.'

LAURA OWEN SANDERSON,
FOUNDER OF WE SWIM WILD

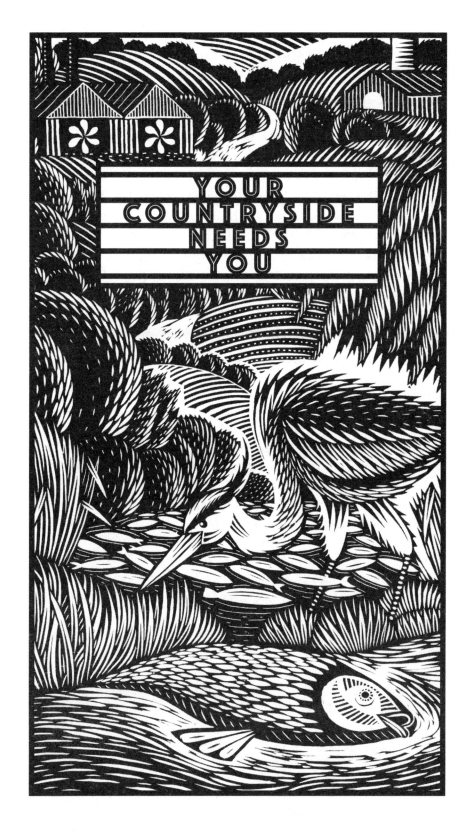

One evening in April 2021, in Little Lever, just outside of Bolton, a hunt saboteur was walking through the woods to check on a local badger sett. That night he found what on all previous nights he'd been guarding against: a group of people, with terriers, spades and crowbars, digging at the sett. Badger baiting has been illegal in England since 1835, but it still happens because it is so hard to police. So, in place of an official defence of the law, it has become regular practice for 'sabs' across England to monitor local setts in their own time, with their own resources. On this occasion, even though he was alone, this sab stepped in between the group of men and the badgers. They beat him with their spades, left him for dead and ran. When he regained consciousness, he found his way to the road and was taken to hospital, where he received forty-two stitches to his face and plastic surgery to repair his ear.

Sabs are all too often portrayed in the media as violent yobs, hell-bent on anarchy. And because the tradition of hunting foxes has historically been the preserve of the aristocracy, those that sabotage it are almost always presented as class warriors, as if protecting a fox being mauled by hounds is an act of jealousy by those that can't afford the trumpets and jodhpurs and horsewhips. Likewise, those that erect treehouses in threatened ancient woodland or burrow under Euston Square to protest against the HS2 rail project are presented, at best, as people who have nothing better to do. But for some people a love of nature is not confined to watching *Blue Planet* on a Sunday night or signing an online petition; it is felt as a familial kinship for the non-human world, something worthy of urgent action. Is it so hard to believe that, when nature does so much for us, people will lay down their lives to protect it?

When the public were expelled from nature, we lost our rights not only to benefit from it, but also to care for it. With private ownership of the land came total dominion of it, and the landowner's 'right to destroy' is a codified legal prerequisite alongside his right to exclude. When we lost our commons, we lost our right to protect nature and, much worse, we almost forgot our collective power and our collective responsibility to stop it being irreconcilably exploited.

One of the arguments against greater public access to nature is that the public can't be trusted, that we represent a danger to ecosystems. But this assertion fails to acknowledge the factor of scale: why do we focus on individuals and ignore the systemic industrialisation of our field systems, which has eliminated the habitat of far more animals than could be crushed by a wanton rambler's boot? It is not the rambler that is devastating our moorland. It is not the wild swimmer who is pouring raw sewage into our rivers. And it is not the protestor who is cutting down our ancient forests. The public are not a threat to the countryside but its last line of defence.

Not everyone can be a tree protestor or a hunt sab. But every week in England, hundreds of thousands of volunteers are working to protect nature in their own ways – from picking up litter and planting trees to campaigning for wildlife. Somehow we have retained our love of nature in spite of being allowed access to so little of it. This chapter looks at some of the myriad ways we can support and protect nature, by ignoring the fences that prevent us doing so, by trespassing.

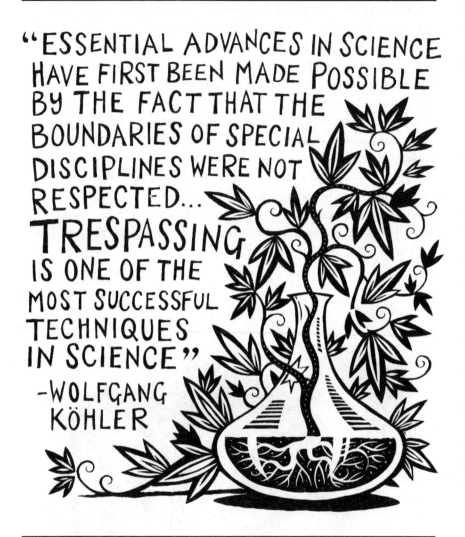

"ESSENTIAL ADVANCES IN SCIENCE HAVE FIRST BEEN MADE POSSIBLE BY THE FACT THAT THE BOUNDARIES OF SPECIAL DISCIPLINES WERE NOT RESPECTED... TRESPASSING IS ONE OF THE MOST SUCCESSFUL TECHNIQUES IN SCIENCE"
—WOLFGANG KÖHLER

Citizen Science

Long before there was science, there was citizen science. The vast infrastructure of expertise that extends over our globe today, the many billions of dollars invested in research, the rigorous template of empiricism that informed the response to Covid-19 – all science originated from the interested lay person, from a simple love of nature.

The process of close observation of the natural world is as old as humans. But the empirical recording, amassing and analysis of data has precedent as far back as two thousand years ago in ancient China, where migratory locusts frequently destroyed harvests. Residents were organised together to track outbreaks, feeding their data to officials. But the phrase 'citizen science' was only coined in the 1990s by Alan Irwin, a sociologist now based at the Copenhagen Business School, who split its definition into two mutual practices: first as the 'science which assists the needs and concerns of citizens', and second as 'a form of science developed and enacted by the citizens themselves'.

Citizen science is no *Dad's Army*. In spite of initial concerns from the scientific community about the reliability of any data that might be collected by inexperienced participants, a vast array of online tools and apps have been created, which both make it easier for the public to participate and standardise the research into usable data. Active public involvement in scientific research has become a global enterprise, growing bigger, more ambitious and more extensively networked by the year. A social networking app called *iNaturalist*, which collates photos sent in by users, has seen its submissions double every year since it began in 2008. Its co-director Scott Loarie estimates that its data has been published and cited in over 150 peer-reviewed papers. Similarly, the Global Biodiversity Information Facility reports that it gets half of its billions of data points from the general public and estimates that it has supplied data for more than 2,500 peer-reviewed papers in the past ten years alone. But citizen science has branched out from just uploading photos. It has been used to monitor pollution, document the spread of mosquito-borne diseases, assess water flow to calibrate flood models and build Geiger counters to study radiation levels.

Its benefits are reciprocal. Citizen science has worked hard to make its projects accessible, fun and exciting, meaning that enacting the process of science can teach a love of science. Like Trash Free Trails reinventing how we relate to litter-picking, there are many schemes designed to make collecting data as exciting as possible. Bioblitzing is just one example, where members of the public come together with wildlife experts and record as many species as they can in a limited timeframe. Just like one-day international cricket, the time limit introduces tension, and by demanding less investment, it introduces a whole new audience to the subject.

Bioblitzes are held all over the world and are often hosted by museums as public-outreach campaigns, involving people in their work and creating hard datasets at the same time. A famous bioblitz was staged in Saguaro National Park, near Tucson, Arizona, where more than five thousand people came together on their hands and knees to study the area. This particular bioblitz lasted twenty-four hours and added more than 400 species to park lists, including 190 species of invertebrates and 205 species of fungus previously unknown to the park. At least one species of plant discovered was new to science.

François Taddei, co-founder of the Center for Research and Interdisciplinarity (CRI) in Paris, thinks there is also a wider benefit of citizen science to society. In his experience, citizen science is a vital means of training society away from our new 'post-truth' zeitgeist. He says that it can revive the practice of critical thinking, saying that children are 'much less prone to fake news and all these problems that we are facing in the information age'.

Science is limited by exclusion. Knowledge is strangled by privatised ownership. With just 3 per cent of rivers accessible to the public and just 8 per cent of land available for study, our ability to observe, record and protect nature through citizen science is hobbled by the archaic laws of trespass. A greater right of public access would allow and encourage a more comprehensive record of the health of our environment.

Invasive Species

Discussions about invasive species can often sound like Nigel Farage guest-presenting BBC Two's *Springwatch*. Words such as 'native' are inextricably tied to politics and ideology, and the insistence on referring to species by their place of origin embeds a pointless nationalism deep into the heart of science, an otherwise borderless realm.

That said, invasive species are a real threat to our nature. They can include parasites, diseases, fungi, plants or animals, and they spread

voraciously, far beyond the habitat they were introduced to. Almost all of them are the result of human intervention, from the mink introduced into England to fuel a fur trade in the 1980s, to ash dieback, a fungus brought to England via the import of saplings. They can eat or parasitise our native species, which, because they did not evolve together, have no defences against them. They can also outcompete native species for food, light or nesting sites, and, like the signal crayfish, can bring diseases for which they have no defences. In short, because they have been transplanted into habitat, they are able to dominate, spread and disrupt the finely tuned balance up and down the food chain.

And the situation is far worse than most people realise. England has over three thousand invasive species, from grey squirrels to knotweed, and they cause such devastation to habitats that a recent report published on the BBC found they are an even bigger threat to biodiversity than climate change. Fifty years ago, Dutch elm disease, a fungus carried on the wings of the elm bark beetle, destroyed millions of English elms, and today, ash dieback now threatens 95 per cent of all ash trees across Europe. Those concerned that none of this might spur our government into action will be glad to hear that invasive species also cost the English economy £1.3 billion, which means people in high places have learned to care.

According to the Natural History Museum, by far the most important step in controlling invasive species is identifying them, locating them and monitoring their spread. The Natural History Museum advises the public to record their observations on the app *iRecord*, which is plugged into several national databases, allowing researchers and conservationists to monitor any changes. But they also advise people not to deal with the invasive species themselves, presumably because, unless they own the land, they don't have the right to destroy them.

But if we're not actually allowed to walk into our woods or to dip into our rivers, the very real effect is that we know much less about the health of our countryside and the spread of invasive species than we should. If the general public, armed only with iPhones, apps and a love of nature, were allowed to access that nature, we could become the ears and eyes of our countryside, protecting it by simply observing and recording.

TAKE ACTION FOR ACCESS

Get into citizen science:
download one of the apps opposite and go explore.

Trespass to conduct your own citizen-science survey of the land. Tell people about it on social media using the hashtag #trespassscience.

CITIZEN SCIENCE APPS

A Partial Introduction

AquaInvaders

Aims to collect much-needed data on freshwater aquatic invasive species around the UK.

Asian Hornet Watch

Enables the recording and early detection of Asian hornets.

British Cellar Spider Survey

British Arachnological Society survey of British cellar spiders.

Crab Watch

Developed to allow you to both learn about and submit records of the crab species around Europe.

Garden BirdWatch

Designed to find out how, when and why birds and other animals use our gardens.

iBats

Monitors bat populations globally by listening to the sounds bats use to navigate and find food.

iRecord

Involves the public with biological recording, contributing species sightings with GPS data, descriptions and other information.

Lichen App

Assess the status of nitrogen in your area by surveying lichen on trees, giving you an estimate of how polluted your area is.

Mammal Mapper

Enables you to record signs and sightings of mammals in the UK.

Rare Arable Flowers

Aims to support UK-wide monitoring of this important group of species, and thus help to inform efforts for their conservation.

That's Invasive!

Lets you identify and record thirty-five different invasive species by utilising your phone's in-built GPS and camera.

Treezilla

An ambitious project to map all of Britain's trees and record data about diseases and the environmental benefits that trees provide.

Zooniverse

A platform for people-powered research, made possible by volunteers who come together to assist professional researchers.

PROTECTING NATURE

Another of the main arguments against greater public access to nature is that we cannot be trusted not to harm the delicate ecology of the countryside. The cry comes up from the land lobby, 'You'll crush the ground-nesting birds!' and with it, a silent exhortation to wilfully ignore a mountain of overwhelming, peer-reviewed scientific evidence. Birds in Europe, generally, are on a steep decline. A paper published by the British Ecological Society in 2020 reported a Europe-wide decline of ground-nesting birds by 74 per cent between 1970 and 2016. But, *quelle surprise*, the actual cause of decline is not Norwegian and Swedish right-to-roamers wantonly stomping on eggs, but, of course, the devastating dominance of industrial agriculture. From the report:

> **Many European breeding bird populations are in decline.
> The causes of these declines reflect recent anthropogenic
> impacts, many driven by agriculture, and studies have focused
> on the effects of agriculture and other forms of habitat
> loss, degradation and fragmentation, invasive species and
> climate change ... The change to agricultural policy across
> Western Europe has intensified food production systems and
> has negatively affected the coexistence of agriculture and
> biodiversity. A particular focus has been on the impact of
> such habitat changes on bird populations and the continuing
> declines despite the use of conservation instruments.**

The lazy cliché of the public as vandals rests on an implicit pretence that care for our environment is a genetic component of owning it. As if

the scientists who wrote the report for the British Ecological Society, all its members, the wider British science community, and all of the citizen scientists, amateurs and enthusiasts of this nation are all vandals because none of them own significant swathes of England.

Beneath the din of cries about ground-nesting birds, there is a quiet, unacknowledged truth. The system of exclusive dominion given to landowners is responsible for the decimation of the environment on a much larger scale than anything the rambler or wild swimmer could enact. No one states this truth because the wrath and rage of the landowner lobby is at such a constant pitch that to match an accusation with an accusation simply pours petrol on the fire. But for a clear-headed conversation about the health of our nature, we must acknowledge a simple, unacknowledged truth: the devastating scale of our habitat loss is enacted by the very system that excludes us from it.

Only if we, the general public, claim our rights of access can we fulfil our responsibility to the environment. With more boots on the ground, more eyes along the hedgerow, more bodies in the water, we can protect nature from the crimes committed against it and learn to care more about the acts that should be criminalised.

UK BIRD POPULATIONS IN STEEPEST DECLINE:

SPOTTED 77% FLYCATCHE

TURTLE DOVE 71%

SONG 56% THRUSH

71% STARLING

WILLOW TIT 78%

So, for an even debate about how to care for the countryside, we need to consider the crimes against nature and the public that are enacted by landowners. Below is a list of some of the crimes you can look out for, and details for whom to contact.

Blocking Up Rights of Way

Section 137 of the Highways Act (1980) is titled 'Penalty for Wilful Obstruction'. It states: 'If a person, without lawful authority or excuse, in any way wilfully obstructs the free passage along a highway he is guilty of an offence and liable to a fine not exceeding [Fl Level 3 on the standard scale].' Public footpaths and public bridleways are shown as green dashes on Ordnance Survey's Explorer maps and red dashes on their Landranger maps. It is illegal to obstruct them. If the path is blocked deliberately, it's a criminal offence, and farmers or landowners can face a fine and a criminal record.

If the path is overgrown from below, it's the local highway authority's responsibility, so call them and report it. You can find who your local authority is by going online (gov.uk/find-local-council). If it's overgrown from the sides, it is the responsibility of the adjoining landowner, but you should still complain to the highway authority. If your right of way is blocked, it is your legal right to use a reasonable alternative path, as long as you don't then enter onto the land of a third party.

Because of another inexplicable addendum to the CRoW Act, the result of bartering our rights away to landowner lobbyists, the government have agreed to an arbitrary cut-off date for registering old rights of way. The Ramblers have identified 49,000 miles of paths across England and Wales that could be lost for ever, unless we come together to save them. So they have produced a guide called 'Don't Lose Your Way', which shows you how to register pathways. Head to the Ramblers website (ramblers. org.uk) to find out more. However, as it stands, to save these paths, the Ramblers will have to identify thirty-three miles of footpath per day for the next four years, which is an impossible task. So, more realistically, when the inevitable campaign starts to push back the cut-off date, please support it.

Fly-Tipping

The extant laws on fly-tipping are unquestionably unfair on landowners. If a landowner is a victim of someone else fly-tipping waste onto their property, it is their duty to pay for it to be removed. This is clearly not just, but it does make sense: if the council were to guarantee its removal, it might encourage people to fly-tip more.

Fly-tipping is a serious criminal offence and can be punished with a maximum fine of £50,000 and twelve months in prison, but people get away with it because it is nigh on impossible to police. In 2016–17 more than 1 million incidences of fly-tipping were dealt with by councils in England, with an estimated cost of over £58 million.

If you see someone fly-tipping, remember it is a crime with a large, life-changing punishment, so the perpetrator will likely be defensive, making it dangerous to confront them. Instead, take note of the date, time and place of the incident, what the waste looks like and how much there is, and descriptions of any person and/or vehicles involved along with the registration number. Then report the incident immediately to the local authority.

Reporting dumped waste on someone else's land will inevitably lead to the landowner forking out tonnes of money, so they will also not be best pleased. But it is precisely for this reason that so much fly-tipped waste gets left in our countryside for so long, and if we are to tackle the issue of litter in the countryside, we must also face this issue head on. In a future England of general public access, the ideal solution would be to call in the commoners to help remove the waste – human chains and hard graft, working to protect nature. But until then, the chances are that landowners will not respond kindly to your concern. However, more consistent reporting of fly-tipping will lead to a greater impetus for landowners to lobby for a different solution, which is vital, because the current laws are first, unfair, and second, unsustainable.

Flailing and Netting Hedges in Nesting Season

It's against the law to intentionally disturb a bird's nest during nesting season (usually March to August). Nevertheless, some farmers and landowners persist in flailing hedges far too late in the spring, after birds have started nesting. There is an excellent online guide from the RSPB about the law around hedgerows being cut during nesting season, which contains numbers to call to report such crimes; just search online using the search terms 'RSPB hedge-cutting law'.

Because landowners and developers aren't allowed to cut or remove a hedge during nesting season, some have started putting nets over hedges to stop birds nesting there in the first place. The best place to find out more is the 'Nesting Not Netting and Other UK Wildlife Crimes!' Facebook page, with over 13,000 members. They'll tell you more info about hedges being netted, where the law stands on this and how to stop it.

Grubbing Up Old Hedges

The Hedgerow Regulations (2006) state that a landowner is not meant to get rid of hedges over thirty years old and more than twenty metres long, but hardly anyone is checking whether they do. If you go trespassing, keep an eye out for any obvious signs of hedgerows being grubbed up (dug up by the roots) and keep notes. For more details, head to the UK government's website (www.gov.uk) or google 'countryside hedgerows protection and management'. This page will also give you contact details if you wish to report a suspected hedgerow offence.

Ploughing Up Ancient Meadows

Industrial agriculture has destroyed some 97 per cent of our wildflower meadows since the 1930s. However, if you do happen to see grassland being ploughed up, it doesn't necessarily mean that a crime is being committed, because this a fairly normal part of agriculture – converting pasture into arable land or cultivating a pasture to reseed it with new grass. However, if you know the field was previously full of wildlife, then it should be reported. Equally, if on inspection the pieces of turf left over after the ploughing appear to have lots of different kinds of wild plants in them, then it is possible that a crime has been committed. If a landowner wants to plough up a pasture, remove scrub or clear historic features, they have to abide by the Environmental Investigation Agency's regulations. One way you can find out where ancient flower meadows are is by looking on the government's MAGIC Map (magic.defra.gov.uk).

River Pollution

There are various telltale signs that indicate your river is in trouble. Untreated sewage pouring from outfall pipes is one clear example. If you notice sewage solids, toilet paper, condoms and sanitary products, soap suds or a milky-looking discharge, grey-coloured water or noticeable sewage smells, that probably means one of the UK's 17,684 licensed sewer overflows is discharging raw sewage directly into the river.

In 2019 there were over 200,000 discharges of untreated sewage into UK rivers. If you see a sewage incident, take note of what you saw, when and where you saw it (including a postcode, road name or any local landmarks or features) and report it to the Environment Agency (0800 80 70 60). Also, if your previously clean and clear river suddenly becomes turbid and muddy, it means there has been lots of ploughing in the catchment area and all the sediment is pouring off the land. In theory this is a breach of the Good Agricultural and Environmental Conditions (GAEC) – a set of EU rules concerning the spreading of slurry or cultivating crops within the buffer strip along rivers and streams – but this is almost never sanctioned.

Pheasant Releases and Their Impact on the Environment

Pheasants are a non-native game bird species to the UK, and the science increasingly shows they're having a growing impact on our

ecosystems, from the structure of hedgerows to the adders that pheasants will attack. Yet every year 47 million pheasants are released by landowners into the countryside for shooting. The environmental campaign group Wild Justice have been challenging the UK government over the legality of this; they found that there hasn't even been an environmental impact assessment for all the thousands of pheasants released near nature reserves. You can join their mailing list and chip in to support their work at wildjustice.org.uk.

Moorland Burning

Every year, between October and April, a small elite of grouse-moor owners light fires on our largest carbon store – our moorland peat bogs. Moorland burning is done to intensively manage heather in order to maximise the number of grouse on a moor for shooting. But doing this also dries out the peat, releasing carbon into the air, and reduces its ability to retain floodwaters in winter. Thanks to pressure from campaigners, a partial ban on moorland burning has recently been introduced, but it's full of loopholes and needs policing by us citizens – as does the rife persecution of birds of prey by grouse-moor gamekeepers. If you live near a grouse moor, you can join a local Moorland Monitors group (moorlandmonitors.org) and help record instances of moorland burning and illegal raptor persecution.

Laura Owen Sanderson

Founder of weswimwild.com

I grew up on the Welsh coast in a place called Harlech. Swimming was in my blood: my mum used to dive for her county, and I have fond memories of my grandfather tying one end of a rope to his waist, the other to a dinghy, and hauling my sister and I to Shell Island and back. From the age of two onwards, we spent our lives in the sea, from March to October. But as I grew older, I lost my connection to the water. I got a job as an art teacher, had a daughter, life took over and I forgot about swimming.

But then, out of nowhere, I got very sick, very quickly. I collapsed at work, was rushed to A & E and I remember thinking, very calmly, that this was it, I was dying. I was almost right. I emerged from a coma to a series of blood transfusions, and as I was recovering, I noticed that my body was really stiff. I could hardly get up in the morning to go to the toilet. Not one doctor could explain it, and I was starting to panic, thinking, I'm not going to be able to do my job any more. How can I raise my kid like this? Then one day, during another series of tests, a trainee doctor suggested that cold-water showers might help. She said that though there was very little in the way of evidence back then, she still reckoned it was worth trying. I instantly thought, No way, I'm a long hot bath sort of person. No way am I ruining my showers. And then I remembered the sea.

So, this was the start of winter, and I just plunged in. I'm not joking: it worked straight away, the stiffness in my joints went away and I was hooked. But as winter drew in, the tides got stronger, and I retreated to the mountains for my swims – the lakes and rivers. That was when the outdoors really took hold of me. I had a real sense of being immersed in nature, not just looking at it, but really being a part of it.

Every day going to the beach had made me realise just how much plastic waste there was on the shore. I thought I ought to do something about it, so I set up the Snowdonia Beach Clean, which was hugely popular, with about eighty people turning up each week. That was great, but even at the start of it I knew that picking up litter isn't the answer. I'd been reading about plastic, about how it never really goes away, but just gets smaller and smaller, until it is invisible but no less present in the world. And I started to wonder about the lakes and rivers up in the mountains.

I decided to swim the length of the River Glaslyn, from the source on Snowdon to the mouth at Porthmadog (about sixteen miles), and I wanted to test for microplastics along the way. Just by chance, a week before I did it, I read about a scientist called Christian Dunn ,who had recently tested the water in ten lakes around the UK with Friends of the Earth. I got in touch with him, and he said it was highly unlikely that I'd find any plastics in the source of the Glaslyn, but he was happy to help me test the samples. It took me two days to swim that river, camping out on the bank overnight at Gwynant. Of course, we found significant amounts of plastics in the water, even at the source, and only a month later a study was released saying how scientists had found microplastics in the air above the Alps. Turns out, invisible microplastics are prevalent in the air and the water: we breathe about a credit card's worth of plastic into our lungs every week. It comes from synthetic fabrics in our washing machines, from car tyres rubbing on the tarmac and from larger plastic waste, which degrades over time.

I thought, I'm going to these pristine places and still they're riddled with plastic. So I took it further and swam all the rivers that cut through UK national parks, the most protected landscapes in our country. On top of the microplastics, I was physically shocked by the filth in the water. I saw sanitary towels in the Derwent. I swallowed chicken shit in the Wye. The Dart and the Beaulieu were gross with sewage overflows, and I got really ill from agricultural run-off and cow slurry. I was there to test for microplastics, but found these rivers were just full of shite.

All the while, I was encouraging people to test their own local waters. We were asking them to fill four sterilised wine bottles and send them in to Christian and his volunteer PhD students, who would test them for microplastics. We were inundated with wine bottles, and a year later the wonderful students are still testing them, compiling the results. But it was so laborious. I was paying for everyone's postage, and it was nowhere near the scale we needed for really useful results. So in 2022, we're upping the infrastructure, looking at setting up local hubs where we can train people to test the water themselves. We're looking for local businesses to stump up the £3,000 to pay for kits and then asking people to come in one day a month to test the water themselves. What we've found with our 'Waterloggers' is that people are genuinely interested in helping improve the health of our rivers, and if you encourage people to do the science themselves, then they're genuinely invested.

But of course, the most important people to engage are our children. We've set up an organisation called Pobl Dwr (Water People), where we take kids to the coast for an immersive science experience. We all got the qualifications to actually take the kids into the sea, to snorkel around the rock pools and see for themselves the life of the shoreline. It's one thing to stand and point at the sea, but to look under the water, to actually be in that environment with the sea life – that's a totally different experience. It takes their breath away, and they instantly fall in love with the coast. We take samples up onto the beach, where we have a mobile science lab. The kids dress up in goggles and white coats and test the water for microplastics themselves, shining a UV light through it, counting the microplastics and then feeding the data back to the lab.

I think there is a serious disconnect between the practice and knowledge

TAKE ACTION FOR ACCESS

Don't wait around for the government to protect our rivers – go out there and do it yourself.

Go online at weswimwild.com/waterloggers and research how you can test the water quality of your local blue space.

There are also tips on how to raise the money yourself to buy a water-testing kit for your local community, so you can collate data from around your region and feed it back to a centralised source.

of science and average people: it's one thing to tell people about microplastics, but for them to see it for themselves is another. It's immersion again – the impact is so much more ingrained. On top of everything else, we are showing these kids the power they have to actually do it themselves, to study the environment and change the world.

DESIGNATING NATURE

In December 2020 a small group of residents in Ilkley, North Yorkshire, made history. After only two years of campaigning, they won EU-designated bathing status over a small stretch of the River Wharfe, which means that sewage discharge is monitored, and there are consequences for overspill. In France, over 500 rivers have been designated with EU bathing status, but until this moment, only the English coastline was protected by this designation. Not only has this group won the right to protect their local river, they have prised open the door, making it easier for groups all over England to do the same thing.

In 2020, water companies across the United Kingdom discharged raw sewage into our rivers over 400,000 times, amounting to a continuous flow of more than 3 million hours. In Ilkley, the campaign produced figures from Yorkshire Water, which showed that in 2019 the Ilkley sewage works discharged raw sewage into the river on 114 days of the year. Even in dry, low-flow conditions, the river below the iron footbridge was showing contamination forty times higher than limits set by the Environment Agency on bathing-water quality, and in wet weather it was as much as fifty times higher.

By showing that on hot days over a thousand people used the river for recreation, the Ilkley Clean River Group were able to demonstrate a public-health necessity for cleaner water. As they say on their website: 'We are a group of Ilkley residents who decided to do something when we saw the state of the river in the summer of 2018. Even though the issue has been going on for years we decided to have one more go to get it sorted.'

The Ilkley campaign was a coalition of groups and individuals who, in the world of property rights, have often been pitted against each other. But when focused not on our rights to the river but our responsibilities to it, anglers, wild swimmers, wildlife enthusiasts, local scientists and residents were able to work together to improve the health of the river. By listening to the perspectives of every invested member of the community, the Ilkley campaign formed a commons to protect their river. But crucially, they were only able to win by

asserting their rights of access in defiance of the laws that banned them from the river – in other words, by trespassing.

Through their efforts in Ilkley, they have helped others' efforts elsewhere. Warleigh Weir, just outside of Bath, will be next in line, with a campaign fuelled by its owner, Johnny Palmer, and the five hundred or so volunteers he has recruited as guardians of the site. Similarly, there are applications pending from the London Waterkeeper for various sections of the Thames, and in Oxford, whose city council recently backed a motion for the Isis to be designated.

The Ilkley Clean River Group's website has morphed from a centralised place to gather names for a petition to a comprehensive resource to aid those who wish to do the same for their river. Any off-putting sense of the grandness of the task, the daunting mountain of admin and unpaid work, is completely dispelled by the chatty, warm tone of the website and the clarity of its experience and advice. There are blogs explaining how the Ilkley residents went about their campaign, downloadable displays of the letters to and from the ministers of the environment and a video, recorded from a live webinar, explaining how to do it yourself.

The campaign is clear about their focus and methods. They advise readers to first pursue the local water authority that governs the rivers and the Environment Agency through the formal routes of their town council or MP, asking them to account for the pollution and take action as the appointed custodians of our rivers. Then they advise close monitoring of water quality

The river Wharfe at Ilkley

and sewage activity when it rains, and more reporting of pollution to the Environment Agency. And they even advise on the communications strategy – how to provide stories to the media that snag the public interest and create momentum.

An example list of advice from the website is so succinct in its wisdom that it serves not just as an activist's handbook, but a mantra for a life well-lived:

1. **Start with understanding what's really going on.**
2. **Be clear about what we are going to achieve.**
3. **Use diversity as a strength – making the most of everyone's views.**
4. **Work with the powers we have locally.**
5. **Bring agencies' accountability to their front door.**
6. **Turn up the heat so no one can walk away.**
7. **Use language that describes reality.**
8. **Build relationships for the task – sometimes collaborative, sometimes adversarial.**

If there is one overriding conclusion to be taken from all this, it is very simple: it can be done. You don't have to identify as an anti-establishment radical to protect your rivers, but nor do you need anyone's permission: you just have to do it. And one final point: you can't do it on your own. Find a group or set one up. Connect with people to connect with nature.

TAKE ACTION FOR ACCESS

Search online for the website Is My River Fit to Play In, an interactive map that allows you to type in the name of your local river, and find out how many times raw sewage has been dumped in it during the last year.

Check out the Ilkley Clean River Group website (ilkleycleanriver.uk) and consider if you'd like to be involved in something similar for your local river.

In the absence of anyone having done so already, set up a 'Friends of the River' group. Whether it be a WhatsApp group, Facebook page or website, set it up, tell people about it, and as anyone in Ilkley will tell you, people will sign up and want to help.

If none of the above is for you, no worries – just contact the Environment Agency (0800 80 70 60) every time you see sewage discharge in the river. Each report will add not just to the incremental evidence of abuse, but also to the story that we, the public, are watching.

DECLARING THE RIGHTS OF NATURE

But we could, of course, go one step further. One midsummer evening in 2021, a group of about a hundred local residents gathered around the banks of the River Cam to declare the rights of the river and pledge to do what they could to peacefully uphold them. Some speeches were made, some photos were taken, and it was all wrapped up in an hour. In one sense, their small gathering was a quaint gesture, parochial, largely ignored by the nation, and in another sense, it was the most radical revision of our relationship to the natural world since the Industrial Revolution. It was probably both.

Lawyers for Nature, who organised the event alongside Friends of the River Cam, said of the event:

> **If the rights of nature are brought into being in the UK, the words and actions of ordinary nature defenders will likely have played a large role in making it so ... The declaration had, at the same time, no effect and potentially huge effects. In technical legal terms it made no difference – the law relating to the river remained the same after the declaration. But, if some of those reading the declaration last night begin to take whatever peaceful steps they can to uphold the river's rights, the practical effects could be huge.**

The campaign to give nature fundamental legal rights of its own, above and beyond the rights of those who own it, began half a century ago, with a paper published in the *Southern California Law Review*. Authored by law professor Christopher Stone, it described how the existing structure of law gave no rights to nature in and of itself, and that changes should be made to give trees and rivers 'legal standing'. In 1989, Professor Roderick Nash published *The Rights of Nature: A History of Environmental Ethics*, in which he explained how, throughout history, the right-less – slaves, women, migrants – have struggled to expand the state's body of legal rights to include themselves. His book made the case for expanding the notion of rights into nature.

In 2006, Tamaqua Borough in Pennsylvania became the first place in the United States, and the world, to give nature formal constitutional rights, and two years later, Ecuador became the first nation to recognise the rights of nature in its constitution. In 2010, Bolivia submitted a 'Universal

Declaration on the Rights of Mother Earth' to the UN General Assembly for its consideration. In 2012, the National Government of New Zealand reached an agreement with the Whanganui River Iwi, the local Māori people, to recognise a legal persona for the Whanganui River. And, as a direct consequence of the declaration at the River Cam, on 12 July 2021 the notion of the rights of nature was first raised in the Houses of Parliament. Green Party peer Natalie Bennett stood up in Prime Minister's Questions and called on the government to show a similar level of concern for our rivers as local communities such as Friends of the River Cam.

And the local communities are central to the efficacy of the rights of nature. For a river to have legal personhood, like a child, a ship or a corporation, it must be represented by a coalition of humans. These humans work to protect the sustainability and health of the river, and would be called upon to speak for the river in court. This structure of responsibility is, again, sourced in indigenous tradition. In New Zealand, rights of nature jurisprudence draws heavily on the Māori philosophy of *kaitiakitanga* or 'guardianship', which views humans as stewards, rather than owners, of the environment. In te reo Māori, *kai-* means 'person who takes action', and *tiaki* means 'to guard, preserve, nurture and protect'. The *kaitiaki* are individual guardians of nature, appointed by the community, and it is their job to represent the best interests of the resource. Depending on climatic and seasonal fluctuations, they limit the amount that locals can use the resource, with the primary aim of keeping it sustainable and healthy, both from the perspective of humans and from that of every other living thing that relies on it. This concept of citizen guardianship is not so alien to us in England.

In fact, we already have a word for it, a word that describes the duties and responsibility that individuals have to their community and land, but whose meaning has become toxified by class politics: *commoner*.

If we are to declare the rights of every river in England, first, every river in England needs its own group of *kaitiaki* or commoners. This is not as difficult as it sounds. The traditions of commoning give rights to those that exercise their responsibilities, which means if you care deeply enough in the cause, if you are willing to dedicate your time and efforts to protecting the river, you need no law or higher authority to authorise a group – you just have to do it.

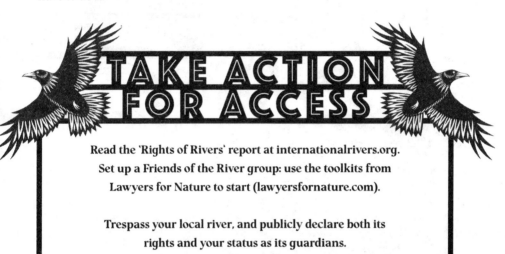

TAKE ACTION FOR ACCESS

Read the 'Rights of Rivers' report at internationalrivers.org.
Set up a Friends of the River group: use the toolkits from
Lawyers for Nature to start (lawyersfornature.com).

Trespass your local river, and publicly declare both its
rights and your status as its guardians.

*The River Cam
at Grantchester
Meadows*

The Responsibilities of *Kaitiaki*

Protecting and upholding the *mana* of the local Māori people – the act of *kaitiakitanga* is a direct expression of their *tino rangatiratanga* or absolute authority

———

Assuring the sustainability of *taonga* (treasures), which includes all natural resources

———

Protecting the delicate balance of ecosystems

———

Assuring that *kaimoana* (seafood) and other *kai* (food) sources will be available for future generations

———

Planning commercial developments with *iwi* (tribes) and Māori leaders who favour harmony within the community and who want to work and move as one

———

Developing educational programmes to explain the interrelatedness between *taonga* (such as seabeds, lands, foreshores, water, air, animals and human beings) and how the degradation of one aspect of *taonga* can seriously affect others

'There was a grace and a beauty in these chalk hills round here in them days. But now you look down there, and all you see is 'ouses 'ouses 'ouses...'

JOHN COPPER,
MEMBER OF THE SUSSEX SINGERS

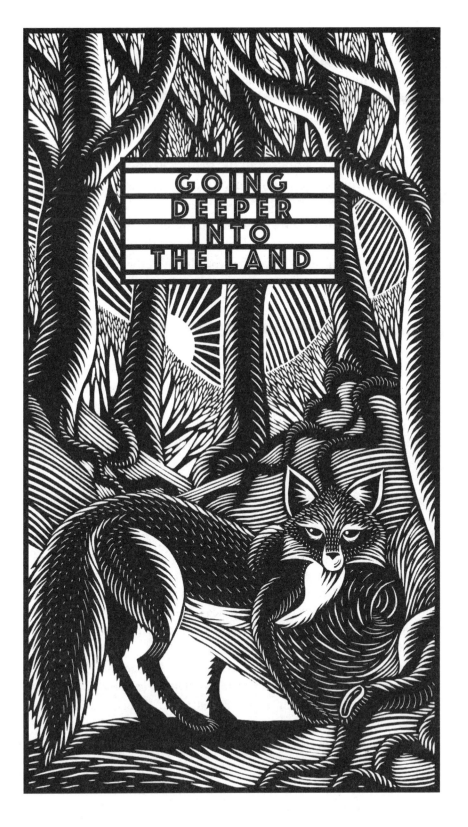

GOING
DEEPER
INTO
THE LAND

L and is a broad term. Our idea of the land encapsulates more than just the soil or topography of a place: it is the history, the ecology and the politics the soil sits in, the societies and cultures it once played host to. Land is the bedrock of society.

To go deeper into the land is to understand more about the society we live in, to situate it in the historical lineage of how people once connected to nature and to understand more about the impact of being estranged from it. For those that own it, land is the basis of their wealth, the bankable solid mass that gives surety to their investments and loans, the mining, farming and forestry of the common resources that formed the rootstock of their inherited power.

To understand how the countryside around us actually works, we need to know about the ownership of land, the commerce and industry related to it, the grants, subsidies and tax breaks we pay for, and what kind of countryside they generate. But we also need to find ways to remember the older relationship we had with the land, a relationship based not on ownership, but on belonging, to reconnect with a past that celebrates the interwoven histories of society and nature, one that also paves the way for a more sustainable, reciprocal future.

THE OWNERSHIP OF LAND

In terms of public access alone, it's not hugely important to know who owns the land; as long as you are respectful of the ecology and don't interfere with the working of the land, then what difference does it make whose name is on the paperwork? It is only the legal fictions sellotaping the laws of exclusive ownership together that make it personal: trespass is defined as a direct and personal attack on the personhood of the owner (whose property is considered an extension of their body). The fact that this bears no resemblance to the actual act of trespass – that, for example, swimming a stretch of the River Loddon in Hampshire causes no actual harm to the Duke of Wellington – doesn't stop this legal fiction barring us from the nature we need so badly.

But as an element of the campaign to open up public access, knowing who owns the land can be a useful component of the narrative. It reveals the history and politics that had the land enclosed in the first place, and puts it into the context of the owner's portfolio of assets, which can often be vast. The Duke of Buccleuch's plans to cut down ten acres of woodland in Kettering to make way for five new warehouses may on its own seem like profit-driven ecocide, but when you learn that the duke owns a total of 280,000 acres across the UK, this raises questions concerning how much more profit the duke actually needs from his land, and also, since he has the option, if there are more appropriate places for his construction work.

There is an online resource that lists plots of land and their owners: the UK government's Land Registry. The trouble is, the Land Registry's information, much like the land it describes, has been privatised. There is a charge of £3 per plot to access that information, and there are more than 24 million registered land titles, meaning that to buy them all and build a comprehensive map of ownership in England, you would need at least £72 million to simply access the information.

There are, however, other ways. The website whoownsengland.org, created by Guy Shrubsole in collaboration with the coder Anna Powell-Smith, ecologist Tim Harris and many other volunteers, is not only a portal to much-needed information on England's landownership, but also spells out the ways in which readers can help add to this data. The website contains investigations into Church land, Crown land, moorland, woodland, aristocratic estates, corporate bodies and much more. With a variety of techniques, Shrubsole (an unlikely intersection of Edward Snowden and Bilbo Baggins) has amassed a dataset that lifts the lid on England's inequality of landownership, exposing the statistics on the opposite page. Perhaps even more shocking than these numbers is the fact that even the Land Registry themselves don't know who owns all the land in our country. Some 5.2 million acres, 15 per cent of freehold land

A third of England's
woodlands are owned by
just a thousand landowners.

A third of England and Wales is owned
by companies and corporate bodies.

The Church of England owns
a 105,000-acre property portfolio
worth £2 billion.

Half of England is owned by less than
1 per cent of the population.

in England, is unregistered. This is because it hasn't changed hands since compulsory registration was introduced, and therefore no title deeds have been processed. As the Land Registry themselves have said: 'Much of the land owned by the Crown, the aristocracy, and the Church has not been registered, because it has never been sold.'

Since publishing his book *Who Owns England?*, Shrubsole has been joined by other campaigners and researchers, spawning franchise investigations that add to the overall map of ownership. Who Owns Wales?, Who Owns Norfolk?, Who Owns Oxford? and Who Owns Middleton? are all separate organisations that feed their data into Shrubsole's mothership. Each has used his extensive guides to create cadastral maps of their local areas, drawing on a variety of resources that are all linked from his website, which provides a detailed explanation of how to create a map of ownership in your own area and how best to draw conclusions from the dataset. The techniques involve a level of computer literacy slightly higher than your average email and Wikipedia user, but are a valuable way for those who are comfortable with programming to contribute to a fuller understanding of how land works in England.

Overleaf is a list of resources that can be used to investigate landownership, useful for those who are keen to contribute to the overall cadastral mapping of England.

UNCOVERING WHO OWNS ENGLAND

---

data.gov.uk
A website listing and linking to all the datasets
published by the UK government.

Defra Data Services Platform (environment.data.gov.uk)
The UK government's environmental spatial data catalogue; all mapping
data published by the Department for Environment, Food and Rural Affairs
(Defra), Natural England and the Environment Agency.

MAGIC Map (magic.defra.gov.uk)
A treasure trove of environmental maps run by Natural England.

OS OpenData Downloads (ordnancesurvey.co.uk)
Ordnance Survey remain pretty big obstacles to open data mapping in the
UK, but these are the datasets they've so far made open.

Private Eye's map of offshore landowners in the UK (private-eye.co.uk/registry)
An extraordinary investigation by journalists Richard Brooks and Christian
Eriksson, with a map designed by Anna Powell-Smith.

1840s tithe maps

Some counties have put them online, for example Cheshire (maps.cheshire.gov.uk), East Sussex (apps.eastsussex.gov.uk), Norfolk (historic-maps.norfolk.gov.uk). If they are not online, appointments can be made in an infuriatingly analogue fashion with local councils' records offices.

1910–15 valuation maps

These detailed maps were commissioned by radical Chancellor David Lloyd George as part of his failed attempt to levy a land value tax on big landowners. Just one county, Oxfordshire (oxfordshire.gov.uk), has put them online, but the National Archives in London keep other counties' maps.

Highways Act 1980, section 31(6)

Obliges local authorities to keep a public register of all landowners whose land is intersected by public highways and rights of way.

Local authority asset registers

Every council is now obliged to publish a list of the property they own. Submit a Freedom of Information (FOI) request to your council if you can't find this on their website.

HMRC maps of tax-exempt heritage assets

Some stately homes and their estates are exempt from inheritance tax and capital gains tax if they open themselves up for public access (even if only for a few days every year). HMRC keeps maps of such estates and properties on their website (hmrc.gov.uk), though only as PDFs rather than digital maps.

THE BUSINESS OF LAND

Every field, tree, river, meadow and flower in England is owned. When a landowner looks at a hill, his vision is not just of trees and meadows, but of boundary lines, tax breaks, net yields, profits and losses. Though this may not be the way you like to see nature, it is the overbearing mechanism that determines what happens to the flora and fauna of our countryside. So it's worth understanding this perspective and knowing a little more about the way land is commodified.

Freedom of Information (FOI) Requests

As a result of the Freedom of Information Act 2000, the public now have a 'right of access' to information held by public authorities. The act allows any person in the UK to make an FOI request, and obliges public bodies first to confirm whether it holds the information requested, and second, if it does have the information, to pass it on.

Below is a list of advice from whoownsengland.org for the best way to go about making an FOI request:

Be clear about what you want to find out.

Frame a question and write the request: what organisations and individuals are involved in this information, which departments does it relate to, and be clear about the subject matter and dates within which your request is applicable. If you can, try and phrase the request using searchable terms, as the public body will enter these terms into their own search.

Submit the request to a public body.

Wait twenty working days (keep a log, note down deadlines).

Follow up if you don't hear back within the deadline.

Depending on the response, you might have to appeal. Report it to the Information Commissioner's Office (ico.org.uk), or if necessary, report it to the media.

Here are some organisations to help you on your way:

gov.uk allows you to view documents previously released under FOI, though it's far from comprehensive. Most departments are rubbish at publishing their FOI responses.

FOI Directory (foi.directory) is an invaluable list of all FOI email addresses for public bodies.

Campaign for Freedom of Information (cfoi.org.uk) is the NGO that successfully campaigned for the FOI Act for thirty years, run by the legendary Maurice 'Freedom' Frankel. They sometimes run workshops on how to use FOI law.

The Information Commissioner's Office (ico.org.uk) is an essential source of guidance in using FOI, a place to make complaints and an archive of the commissioner's judgements in past cases.

WhatDoTheyKnow (whatdotheyknow.com) is a popular site for publicly submitting FOI requests. Responses from public authorities are also all published, so it's worth checking to see if the information you want has already been released before.

There is no need to be put off either by formality or by the implications of your request. As of 2000, this information is your right, and public bodies have a legal duty to provide it. Your request doesn't have to be anything more than a couple of lines. For example, when the Right to Roam campaign was investigating the government's woefully lacklustre promotion of the

Countryside Code, the FOI request came in the form of a very simple email from Guy Shrubsole, quoted below:

> Would you be able to also send me what the budget for promoting the Code has been to date? If the figures exist, going back to 2004 ideally (I think that's when it got a reboot to accompany Right to Roam coming into effect)? Or if those historic figures aren't to hand – just for the past couple of years?
>
> Thanks and best wishes,
> Guy

When Natural England, the government body in charge of the Countryside Code, got back to Shrubsole, they provided the costings, as requested. And a few telephone calls later, these figures became a national news story. An article in the *Guardian*, for example, opened:

> An unprecedented rise in litter, damaging fires and 'fly-camping' across the English countryside is partly a result of the government spending less than £2,000 a year over the past decade on promoting the Countryside Code, campaigners say.

From this one email, Shrubsole was able to create a story, uncover new information and set out a more complex picture of systemic failings that led to the litter problem in England. It also allowed him to bring the campaign's ethics to a wider audience. In the same article, Shrubsole said:

> Access to nature is vital for everyone's mental and physical health, and it's brilliant to see more people visiting the countryside this year – the vast majority of whom treat it with respect. But the government shares some responsibility for the awful recent instances of littering and vandalism through their consistent failure to promote the Countryside Code.
>
> In other European countries, greater freedom to access nature comes hand-in-hand with a culture of 'leave no trace'. The government ought to be fostering that here, by extending our existing right to roam alongside a properly funded public information campaign on responsible access.

Information on Companies

How do we know that the company that is financing the controversial third runway at Heathrow is the same company that is profiting off the felling of trees in Sheffield? How do we know that Wessex Water, which controls the input of sewage into the River Avon, is owned by YTL Corporation Berhad, an infrastructure conglomerate based in Malaysia, with revenues of around $4 million? Simple: we research council documents and follow the money.

Such investigations lend strong plausibility to the notion that our treasured English flora and fauna are being carved up or poisoned for the benefit of the shareholder profits of obscure, shady national and international corporations. Such allegations are often dismissed as bunkum by those perpetrating ecocide, but hard evidence, such as that freely available from the following websites, makes it harder for them to dismiss.

Companies House (beta.companieshouse.gov.uk)

Search and view documentation on every registered company in the UK, their directors and their annual accounts. A great example of how a public-sector organisation can embrace open data for the benefit of everyone.

OpenCorporates (opencorporates.com)

For checking out companies registered overseas or in offshore jurisdictions. A great project promoting transparency, and the largest open database of its kind in the world.

DueDil (duedil.com)

For understanding the relationship between firms and their subsidiaries and parent companies (though be aware you have to pay after a free trial).

Information on Farm Subsidy Payments

More often than not, the woodlands that the general public are banned from, or the green belt they are fenced out of, is paid for by the very people excluded from it. A quick investigation into the subsidies that landowners receive from the public purse make the notion of 'welfare-state scroungers' somewhat ludicrous. For example, in 2015, Britain's twenty-four non-royal dukes received £8.4 million in farm subsidies, which is a lot of money for the negligible work of inheriting land. They also raise the question that, since so much money is being handed to landowners, why are the public systemically blocked from seeing the fruits of their donations? Here is a list of ways to get started researching the murky world of subsidies:

Defra CAP payments (cap-payments.defra.gov.uk)

This website provides a list of all farm subsidy payments

made under the Common Agricultural Policy in each of the nations of the UK, for the years 2015 and 2016. Information from earlier years can still be found on FarmSubsidy.org, an organisation that campaigned for years for greater transparency on this.

Natural England Environmental Stewardship map files
Search 'Environmental Stewardship Scheme Agreements' on environment.data.gov.uk. This information is designed to be viewed in GIS (geographic information system) software like QGIS, a free, open-source app for viewing geospatial data. (NB: the files are very large.)

English Woodland Grant Scheme (EWGS) payments
These subsidies were distributed by the Forestry Commission for the creation and maintenance of woodland. See Guy Shrubsole's blog on whoownsengland.org for a digestible summary of the data. The scheme has expired, but information on the subsidies is still available.

Anna Powell-Smith's online map of Environmental Stewardship maps (farmpayments.anna.ps)
For ease of viewing and searching recipients of the £2.6 billion in grants dished out under Environmental Stewardship scheme.

TAKE ACTION FOR ACCESS

If hopping a fence feels too threatening, if you don't want that nasty cortisol spike of an actual trespass, then there are plenty more ways to contribute to the campaign. Try trespassing the barriers of knowledge that prevent us from understanding the reality of our countryside.

Go to whoownsengland.org to find out how to map your own local area.

Use FOI requests to find out about the land: for example, we know that very few landowners have taken advantage of the legislation to dedicate their land to public access under the CRoW Act, but no-one knows exactly how many, or what the acreage is. This information is freely accessible as a public right, and yet no one has looked into it.

THE SOCIETY OF LAND

The opening track to the *Imagined Village* album, a deeply political work of art that centres the voice and traditional music of diasporas right at the heart of the English folk tradition, begins with a recording of John Copper, a member of a revered family of Sussex singers, who have been performing traditional folk songs for six generations. In a gentle Sussex twang, John quotes his grandad from a 1951 BBC recording:

> **'I still do like to walk up on those old hills, where I was a shepherd boy, but they've changed today, they're all different now,' he said. 'You might see a boy today on a tractor, with his jam and his spam sandwich. Ah,' he said, 'when I was a young man, we had to walk ten mile behind the plough, to plough an acre, and then we'd get home and have a good old hambone and a bit of pork. Yes,' he said, 'it's changed a lot today. When we was up there, we used to look down and all you'd see was that sheep-cropped turf and the lovely curl of the downs. Those lovely curling contours as it goes down to the sea reminded you of a female body. There was a grace and a beauty in these chalk hills round here in them days. But now you look down there, and all you see is 'ouses 'ouses 'ouses...'**
>
> **'That makes me prostrate with dismal,' he said.**

There is an alternate history of the land, one not taught in schools, one not told on the websites of the corporations that own it. It is the people's history of the land, the memories, the struggles and the pleasures of a lived experience in nature. These are the stories of the land and the community, the sincere human love felt for a place, and they convey the emotional side of history, that wrench of seeing loved land disappear under the plans of the developer. They are told in folk songs, in poetry, film and art, but they are also found in conversations with older people.

One of the reasons the Scottish Land Reform Act (2003) was so successful is that their version of the enclosures, the Clearances, were still alive in the cultural memory of the people. But because the main surge of enclosures happened so long ago in England, the visceral feel of the estrangement from nature has long since faded. But there are still people alive today who were children before the ancient character of the English countryside had been defaced by the forces of modern enclosure, industrialisation and neoliberalism. These are the elders of our landscape: the men and women, black, brown and white, queer and straight, who remember our countryside, and our connection to it.

Go seek them out. They will tell you about the watercress meadows they used to forage as children, now cemented over to be a car park for a riverside block of flats; they will tell you how you could barely walk in the fields for all the brown hares and their leverets in April. They'll tell you what the dawn chorus used to sound like in UK woodlands. And these so-called elders don't even have to be that old: ask the average fifty-year-old today what the woods sounded like when they were children, and they'll describe the music of an avian orchestra 30 per cent bigger than it is today.

Older people hold the memory of the land. Across England today, there are countless clubs, societies and organisations set up by local enthusiasts, mainly retired, whose members and websites hold a veritable treasure trove of information that will help you to see the land through different prisms. There are history societies, geological societies, and clubs for entomologists, botanists and archaeologists, who run group events, lectures and walking tours about local areas. Every county has a plethora of groups that meet to discuss their various interests in their landscape. To take West Berkshire as an example, among others there is the West Berkshire Heritage Forum, the Berkshire Archaeological Society, the Berkshire Archaeology

Research Group, the Berkshire Local History Association, Friends of the West Berkshire Museum, the Kennet Valley at War Trust, the Newbury District Field Club, the Newbury Geological Study Group, the Thatcham Historical Society and the Goring Gap Local History Society, not to mention organisations such as Berkshire Botanical Gardens, whose amateur founders did so well that their society became incorporated into a professional organisation.

Not only do these societies provide social companionship for their members, but they also hold valuable source materials such as tithe maps, old maps that predate Ordnance Survey. These are an essential tool for identifying disused rights of way, which in many cases are only being monitored and kept in use by a rare group of individuals who care deeply enough to make it their business. Unsung, unacknowledged, they spend their evenings or their retirement poring over maps, because they know how important these pathways are to their local society, and they know that if they don't take responsibility, no one else will.

To join these societies, or to simply speak to the elders of our land, is to develop a picture of community engagement with the land – the real, lived experience of people who worked and engaged with nature. By better understanding our societal history of the land, we have a clearer picture of its potential for the future, a vision of how community and land could be entwined once again.

Iris Webber

Retiree

I'm ninety-three years old, and I've lived all my life between Dartington and Staverton in Devon. Back in the 1920s, my father was a tree feller, and a champion at that – he won the local cup in Taunton. My grandmother used to wash for the village, and would have to light great fires under bath tubs to boil the water.

We were luckier than most growing up as we had a garden, and my father planted a corner of it with irises, so that was my little corner of the world. I used to play up there, or spend the rest of my time wandering the lanes and the banks of the rivers and streams. We went everywhere on foot, to work or to play, and spent most of our time outdoors. The countryside was our life, the woods and lanes and mud and water, and on Sundays we'd go out for long walks as a family. It was then that we learned what you can and can't touch, what you can and can't put in your mouth. You learned about the life around you, because you saw it every day of the week.

We would never really see the people that owned the land and we didn't get in a lot of trouble, not really. I mean, you always respected the land. We never left gates open, because we knew what would happen if you did – the animals would get out, and be in someone's garden, and then you'd be in a damn sight of trouble. We used to pick the roadside flowers, where there would be hundreds of snowdrops, or go beside the streams to pick primroses, and send them off to London to be sold. Kids aren't allowed to do that these days. People turn round and say you mustn't do this, mustn't do that. Well,

I know for a fact that if you pick the primroses, you get more. This is where you need to know your countryside. You only get one flower to a snowdrop, whereas primroses will shoot more buds – if you pick a few it gives more space for them to come up. You learn it because you live in it.

I left school at fourteen and got a job as a telephonist. Unless you were rich, you didn't get the advantages of college or university. I met my husband, who worked in the estate nursery, planting tree seeds. When we had kids, they would do the same as we did, and be off out for hours on end, playing in the spinneys or the streams. My younger son spent a lot of his time down in the hunt's kennels, cutting up meat for the dogs. In those days, a farmer that had a sheep or cow die on them would call up the hunt, and they would collect it to feed the pack. He's a head chef now.

It's a heck of a lot different these days. There's more cars and more houses, for starters. There's twice the amount of people in the village and just the same amount of shops and the like. Many of the spinneys in the middle of the meadows have been cut down. And unless you're coying in the animals with food and bait, you just don't see the wildlife. One thing I think we've lost is the cuckoo: I don't know when I last heard a cuckoo, but you used to hear them all the time in spring.

And people aren't out and about as much. The landowners don't want people going onto their property, and kids are indoors more generally. My kids used to roam around the ten-acre field at the back of the house. A really beautiful meadow. But the estate has just sold it off to developers, and there'll be eighty houses built there, all for a quick bit of money to keep the estate going. I think the original owners would be turning in their graves. Everybody is just open-mouthed, because we never even dreamed it would happen, but it has happened and that's that.

THE SPIRIT OF LAND

Look up the history of an area of land, and you'll find a long lineage of nobles and peers, what wars they fought in to be awarded the land, how they employed landscape architects such as Capability Brown to stick a hill here and carve a lake there. The story of the land, as it is presented in England, is entirely one of ownership, forever linked to the families and great men who enclosed, inherited or bought it. Their coats of arms still remain on pub signs, their names are given to roads and streets, written into the landscape they've owned for hundreds of years.

But there are countless other tales to tell, folk stories that arise from the commons, from a shared community knowledge of the land. These stories of monsters, ghouls, spirits and giants speak not of landownership, but of a certain kind of belonging, a collective, community understanding of the atmosphere of a place, brought about by experiencing it. They are crucial links to the phenomenology of the landscape, and tell an entirely different story from that of ownership and exploitation.

Stories such as these cannot arise from the mind of one individual; they do not descend from on high, but instead take a community, a shared network of minds, to settle, seed and take root. For some, these stories arise from the weird esoteric mindscape of the people that inhabit them, from a need to imbue the landscape with meaning and a personality of its own. For

The owlman of Mawnan

others, the *genius loci* (spirit of place) is something more elemental: the writer Peter Ackroyd refers to this as a 'territorial imperative', believing that there is something in the character of a landscape that informs the actions and beliefs of those that experience it. He believes that it is the land itself that generates the stories; it merely uses humans to tell it. This spirit, he claims, continues to generate its essence regardless of the efforts of town planners, councils and politicians. But only if its stories continue to be told.

England is riddled with legend. A headless horseman gallops through Folly Wood in Wiltshire. A 'ratman' haunts an underpass in Southend. A man with the face of an owl and huge white wings is spotted only by young girls in Mawnan. There is a spectral lion in Nottinghamshire, and there are dragons in Saffron Walden, Herefordshire, Berkshire, Devon, Somerset and Sheffield, and most famous of all, the Lambton Worm up in Durham, which rampaged through the landscape, munching on sheep and sucking the cows dry of milk. It was eventually slain by a young knight returning from the crusades, who covered his armour in sharp spearheads, letting the dragon crush him in its coils, thereby slicing itself into ribbons.

There are boggarts in Yorkshire, will-o'-the-wisps in Dartmoor, piskies in Cornwall, hickey sprites in Norfolk, the lantern men of Wicken Fen, all manifestations of mischief who tie the best laid plans of men into knots that lead to somewhere between simple frustration and mortal despair. The Bulbeggar is a Somerset boggart who first appeared in the nineteenth century when a farmer stopped to help a fallen figure on the road. As he leaned over the figure to help, it rose from the ground, getting taller and taller, until it towered above him, sending him sprinting homewards in terror. The Bulbeggar remains on Creech Hill in Somerset, cackling through the night, sending shivers down the spines of lone travellers. These boggarts, local to areas, have morphed into the more generic bogeys, or bogeymen, convenient warnings that parents use to keep children from straying too far from home.

The Orford Wild Man, the North Surrey Gigantopithecus, the giants Gog and Magog that form the two sleeping hills just outside of Cambridge – England is stalked by unearthly figures. They aren't always larger than life, though. The Tiddy Mun of Lincolnshire is described as being the size of a toddler but looking like an old man with long, tangled white hair and beard. There are spectral dogs all over England, a black bull called Big Vaughan and a talking mongoose on the Isle of Wight. Some aren't even people or animals, two classic examples being the talking apples of Somerset and the spectral bag of soot that terrorises a road outside of Crowborough, Sussex.

The lantern men of Wicken Fen

Some of England's spirits arise from literature, and have been so popular that they have moved from the pages of fiction, through the minds of their readers, and eventually, free of their books, they haunt the landscapes described by their authors. Ratty from *Wind in the Willows* is one such character, whose lazy-day philosophy has come to reside over the stretch of river from Pangbourne to Cookham. Some legends have taken so strongly that their origin in fiction has been forgotten. The *Man in the Moone* is the first science fiction book to have been written in English. Published in 1638, Francis Godwin's story is set in Woolpit, Suffolk, in the Middle Ages, and tells a tale of little green children sent down from the moon. The image caught on, travelled across the Atlantic, and morphed into the popular 1950s notion of aliens being small, green-skinned men from Mars.

Other stories originate from historical fact, such as Mother Demdike or the Pendle witches up in Lancashire. There is Sally in the Woods, an old woman whose ducking is in the records of Bath, and whose sudden appearance along the A36 has been the cause of eleven car crashes in the last decade, and the Long Meg stone circle, in Eden Valley, Cumbria, formed when a woman and her daughters were turned to stone by God for profaning the Sabbath. Nan Tuk of Buckstead, East Sussex, was fleeing authorities and escaped into the woods, where she remains in spirit form to this day. Likewise, every year, on the anniversary of the Battle of Edgehill, the ghosts of the Roundheads and the Cavaliers rise from the earth to re-enact the battle that laid them there to an uneasy peace.

Some ghouls, especially the water-based legends, serve as health-and-safety warnings. The Grindylow is a water-dwelling bogeyman from Yorkshire and Lancashire, who has long sinewy arms and is famed for drowning children in bogs and pools. Cutty Dyer is an evil fairy who lives by the town bridge in Ashburton, Devon, who pulls people into the river, never to resurface. Peg Powler haunts the banks and beds of the River Tees, grabbing swimmers by the ankles and pulling them under; Peg, in turn, is a local iteration of the ubiquitous Jenny Greenteeth, a green-skinned hag of the North, with an insatiable thirst for drowning any that stray too close to a strong current.

What these stories do is animate a landscape, instil an animus, a spirit, that is known to all who live there, and like Peter Ackroyd's territorial imperative, it resides there in the mindscape of its locals, above and beyond any ownership-based modifications to the landscape. But they also express a commons philosophy that is often contrary to the ideology put forward by the government and media of the time, an ideology that is fiercely defensive of the genius loci that safeguards an area from excessive development and burial under tarmac. For the Victorian writer John Ruskin, the legend of St George and the Dragon became symbolic of local uprisings against industrialisation, development and the carving up of the countryside for personal profit. The slaying of the dragon would return England to its mythical state of Eden. In 1871, Ruskin founded the Guild of St George, a charity for arts, crafts and the rural economy. The

guild was founded on the principles set out in his book *Fors Clavigera*, a collection of ninety-six letters to the 'workmen and labourers of Great Britain'. Inspired by the ancient legend, Ruskin set out a vision of England that defied industrialisation and empowered local communities to remain in close contact with nature. The guild survives to this day, and is now an international organisation that pursues the same ends.

Legends act like a football team, binding its locals to the area. Go to Brentford in West London, and you'll see griffins everywhere. This hybrid of lion and eagle adorns the sign of the Griffin pub and the Fuller's brewery, and lives on in the name of Brentford football team's home stadium. The eponymous griffin, as the story goes, was once a gift from King Charles II to his mistress Nell Gwyn, which she kept in her house in Butts Estate in Brentford. One day, the griffin fell into the River Thames and was presumed drowned. In fact, it had swum to an island in the Thames, Brentford Eyot, where, being a mythical creature, it was able to survive for a century or more on a diet of geese and ducks. In 1771, when Captain Cook returned home from Australia on HMS *Endeavour*, a botanist called Joseph Banks brought with his cargo of specimens an Australian griffin, which was housed in the newly built pagoda of Kew Gardens, just a hundred yards from Brentford Eyot. Their griffins, of course, got it on and Brentford Eyot became home to a colony of the mythical animals.

And that's not the end of it. Griffins live on in the Brentford psyche so strongly that in 1984 a Brentford man was strolling by the Griffin pub on Braemar Road when he saw a strange creature hovering in the sky. Kevin Chippendale reported to the local press that this animal seemed like a dog with the wings and beak of an eagle. His sighting sparked a flurry of similar accounts, which caused such a stir, locally and nationally, that they were featured on the BBC's *Six O'Clock News*.

We are hungry for these tales. They remain like silhouetted rock forms in the landscape, triggering local pride, generating a sense of connectivity, strengthening resistance against the forces of ownership that seek to obliterate their ethics. But for their power to persist, they must be told and retold, reworked by modern imaginations, to suit the needs of the time.

TAKE ACTION FOR ACCESS

Research your own local area, or an area you want to visit, and which spirits and ghouls operate within it.

Head out for a trespass with friends. Find a nice spot on the earth: a shady grove, a bubbling brook, anywhere that is thriving and brimming with wild nature. Sit down and tell the stories of the place.

Better yet, go camping with some friends, light a (safe and responsible) fire and share some stories aloud.

'There's a risk that people will think foraging is all about harvesting free food, that it encourages a selfish attitude. But it's not that. It's not just about us, it's about all of us, human and non-human.'

MARIA FERNANDEZ GARCIA,
FOUNDER OF HEALING WEEDS

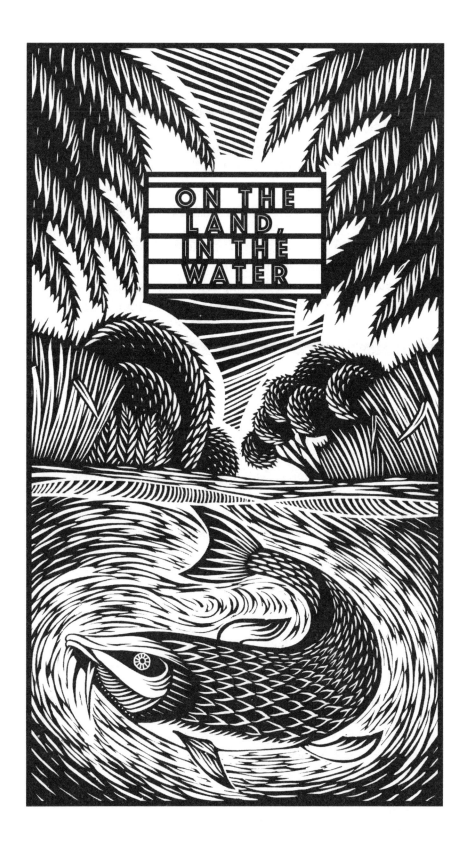

T he lost art of being on the land and in the water is another casualty of enclosure. We have been banned from nature for so long that it is hardly surprising we have forgotten how to treat it with the respect and reverence we owe it. A Catch-22 now confines and defines our relationship with the countryside: the public are excluded from nature because we are told we don't know how to behave, and while we are banned, we have no opportunity of gaining that experience. The rare instances of fires caused by wild camping or the lockdown explosion of litter are used as evidence to feed the myth of a careless general public who couldn't give a damn about the countryside. But if a drink-driving incident doesn't cause all driving to be banned, why should responsible roamers be punished for the acts of the irresponsible?

The Outdoor Swimming Society say as much on their website: 'Outdoor swimming has been outlawed and discouraged for decades, resulting in generations losing knowledge and confidence to participate.' Many people are put off spending the night in nature or swimming in rivers because they haven't grown up doing it. They have never had the chance to learn, with and without supervision of elders; they have never made mistakes and learned from them.

Because these activities are banned, there is no government-endorsed guidance or publicity on how to do them safely, both for the environment and the person. Along with the repressive laws of trespass, the lack of guidance has led to a sense that swimming, camping and laying a fire simply cannot be done without causing damage, and, more subtly, has led to a given assumption that risk is in and of itself a bad thing. The outrage that a member of the public might want to experience nature has infantilised our psyche – we seem to accept that we cannot be trusted.

But there is still a whole host of lived wisdom about how to behave in the countryside. From bushcraft leaders and forest school organisers, to wild campers on Instagram and wild swimming coaches, the general public have amassed a well of knowledge that is useful to all, and not just those affluent enough to be able to purchase the lifestyle experience. Any expansion of our rights of public access and licensed activities would, like every right-to-roam code in existence, come with a detailed guide of the responsibilities we owe nature and its workers.

Walking in straight lines along designated rights of way is not enough. There is so much more to do in nature. Here are some of the activities closely associated with the land and water, imaginative things to do while trespassing, things that forge a deeper connection with the elements and expert guidance on how to do them safely.

WILD CAMPING

The most striking omission from the English Countryside Code is guidance on wild camping. We live in an absurd situation where, because wild camping is illegal, there is no government guidance on how to do it safely. This in itself is logical, because it would be odd for a government to post advice on how to burgle a house safely or get away with murder, but it does leave us in a surreal situation where something that many thousands of people do in nature every year is omitted from the Countryside Code.

Similarly bizarre is the fact that, while it is simultaneously vilified in the press and by landowning associations, much of England's most lauded nature books include accounts of sleeping out in nature. Of course they do: the drama of feeling darkness creep into a landscape, the transition of sights, sounds and smells into night, not to mention the resplendent glory of the rising sun and dawn chorus, makes for good copy. In Robert Macfarlane's *The Old Ways*, a classic meditation on walking the ancient paths that cross our landscape, he breaks the new law of criminal trespass on numerous occasions. One night in particular he sleeps out beneath the beech boughs of Chanctonbury Ring, and wakes to the screeching howl of an ancient and

well-documented ghost. It thrills him with a mixture of fear, adrenalin and wonder, a sensation that connects him to a long lineage of experiencing the haunting effects of a landscape. Yet should his readers wish to emulate him and seek out that ghost for themselves, through the Police, Crime, Sentencing and Courts Bill, they could be punished with three months in prison. While award-winning wordsmithery can grant you access to the backstage area at Hay Festival, it should not be a criterion for experiencing the English countryside.

The British Mountaineering Council have recently stepped into the void left by the government and issued a YouTube guide on how to wild camp safely, while being sensitive to the ecology of the area. As ever, with most guidance on the right and proper way to act in the countryside, it can be summed up thus: don't be a plonker. Be aware of your surroundings, be safe, don't go anywhere near private residences, clear up after yourself, light a fire only when you can guarantee it won't spread, and finally, obviously, leave your disposable barbeque at home. You don't need it.

But to be more precise, here is the Scottish Outdoor Access Code on camping, which has successfully been promoting the responsible experience of sleeping out in nature for the last two decades.

THE SCOTTISH OUTDOOR ACCESS CODE

www.outdooraccess-scotland.scot

Access rights extend to wild camping. This type of camping is lightweight, done in small numbers and only for two or three nights in any one place. You can camp in this way wherever access rights apply, but help to avoid causing problems for local people and land managers by not camping in enclosed fields of crops or farm animals and by keeping well away from buildings, roads or historic structures.

Take extra care to avoid disturbing deer stalking or grouse shooting. If you wish to camp close to a house or building, seek the owner's permission.

Leave no trace by:
Taking away all your litter.
Removing all traces of your tent pitch and of any open fire.
Not causing any pollution.

The Access Code notes that access rights do not apply to motor vehicles. The Code also highlights the risk of impacts due to high levels of use in particular areas.

You need to be aware that while you might visit a place only occasionally and feel that you cause no harm, the land manager or the environment might have to cope with the cumulative effects of many people. Acting with awareness and common sense underpins responsible behaviour.

We would like to add just one further piece of advice, gleaned from years of hard-won experience: wipe your ass with moss, not bog roll. Sphagnum moss beats the hell out of any aloe vera-infused paper you can buy, and it is guaranteed 100 per cent organic. Oh, and bury your poo with a trowel.

LIGHTING A FIRE

Lighting a fire on private property sounds like arson, but building a campfire in nature sounds very nice indeed. The trouble is, in England, they are seen as one and the same thing. A fire that is out of control can be devastating, to nature and humans alike, but a controlled fire is exactly that – there is virtually no risk at all. You light a fire inside your car every time you turn the key in the ignition. The crucial factor is whether the person laying the fire is equipped with the knowledge of how to do so safely, and also conscious of the environmental and weather-related factors specific to its location.

Again, since this is not covered in the Countryside Code, the public have no means of learning how to control a fire in nature, and for the one or two extreme examples of malpractice, the rest of us are banned from making our experience of nature more comfortable and magical.

But we can turn to the Scottish Outdoor Access Code for guidance. The lighting of a fire is allowed as part of the exercise of access rights, if it is done responsibly. The Access Code provides the following guidance, which, notably, demands duties not just of campers but of landowners as well.

FOR CAMPERS

Wherever possible, use a stove rather than light an open fire.
If you do wish to light an open fire, keep it small, under control and
supervised – fires that get out of control can cause major damage, for
which you might be liable.

Never light an open fire during prolonged dry periods or in areas such as
forests, woods, farmland, or on peaty ground or near to buildings or in
cultural heritage sites where damage can be easily caused.

Heed all advice at times of high risk. Remove all traces of
an open fire before you leave.

FOR LAND MANAGERS

At times of drought, work with your local authority (fire services)
to inform people of the high risks involved.

On top of this code, there are a few extra points to bear in mind. When
looking for a spot to lay a fire, make sure you are far away enough from trees
that their roots are not harmed. Before you lay the fire, sweep away dry twigs
and leaves so they don't catch and spread. To be extra sure, line it with stones
(preferably not flint, which explodes at high temperatures) or dig a trench
around it with wet soil. Never cut down wood for fuel, but collect wood that
has fallen to the floor. Ash is by far the most popular wood with fire makers
because, as every woodcrafter knows, ash burns green. This means it doesn't
have to be seasoned for a year (at least) to burn bright, hot and with little
smoke. But it's not hard to find seasoned wood of any kind. Just look for wood
that has fallen on top of other wood, or is caught, hanging in the branches,
left lying there long enough for the sap to dry, but far enough removed from
the damp earth not to rot. Aside from burning with relentless smoke, rotten
wood becomes a lively home for insects, so it's always worth peeling off the
bark of the wood to see if that process has begun. If it has, let the insects be
and find another branch.

Make sure you put out the fire completely before leaving it – piss on it,
pour every last drop of liquid you have on it, and stamp out the embers with
your boots. This may be an ignominious end to a beautiful campfire, but it is
the only way to guarantee the habitat is still there, unharmed, for next time.

WILD SWIMMING

Wild swimming is just swimming outside of swimming pools. Swimming in nature has been so divorced from our lives that its substitute, swimming in chlorinated pools, has become our norm. The hashtag #wildswimming has fuelled the recent popularity of the sport but has also served to reinforce it as something 'other', and as such, has forged a kind of brand that marginalises many people.

Search Instagram with the hashtag #wildswimming and scroll through the hundreds of thousands of images, and you'd be forgiven for thinking that swimming in nature is the sole purview of predominantly white, middle-class, affluent people with toned bellies. This is not the hashtag's fault, or indeed any of the people that post under it, but it is the responsibility of the government to ensure that a sport that could offer such physical and mental health benefits is not only open to all, but that the most marginalised of communities are actively encouraged towards it.

Alongside the laws that ban us from our rivers, lakes and reservoirs, there are several misconceptions about wild water that form a mind wall between the public and nature.

Rivers Are Icky

Rivers *are* icky. First off, there's the goose shit: white-and-green gifts from nature's favourite honkers, splurged onto the riverbank like someone stepped on a tube of toothpaste. Then there's that sucking grey mud in between your toes, and the riverbed farting methane and sulphur up at you as you wade in. Your nose sitting just above the surface, and your mouth ducking in and out of the water as you stroke. Some people are completely put off by these elements of wild swimming; but while some will never be persuaded, most just need to scale the wall of ick, give it a go and realise not just that the benefits far outweigh the negatives, but that the negatives just aren't that bad. Ick is OK.

Much of the wall of ick is built from that deep taboo of disgust, an incremental normalisation of modern sterile environments – clean, smooth surfaces and organised spaces that have made us react viscerally to anything else. Disgust is interesting. For the bioethicist Leon Kass, disgust 'is the emotional expression of deep wisdom, beyond reason's power to fully articulate it'. It is an evolutionary reaction that stops us from eating rotten meat or drinking stagnant water. But for Martha Nussbaum, a legal ethicist, the politics of disgust can inform the way we create society. Writing in *Hiding From Humanity: Disgust, Shame, and the Law*, she argues that the unreliable emotion of disgust supports and propels bigotry, in terms of sexism, racism and judgement of people's sexual orientation. The precepts of the law are based on this irrational, often unsupportable, emotion. Maybe this explains why we have come to accept the razor wire that blocks us from our rivers and reservoirs. Maybe, subconsciously, we feel that the razor wire protects us from the slithering river.

Our rivers are in a filthy state. Even unpolluted rivers can threaten the swimmer with Weil's disease, for example, but these threats can be mitigated by safe swimming. The

billions of tonnes of raw sewage pumped into our rivers – as well as the chicken shit, cow and pig shit, chemical fertiliser run-off and the harmful neonicotinoids leached by insecticides – does raise the chances of the wild swimmer getting ill from swallowing river water. But as long as you take precautions, as long as you don't swim after excessive rainfall (when the sewerage discharges the most), as long as you check for indicators of pollution, like scum on the stones, or thick, greasy water viscosity, there is very little chance of illness or disease.

Just to be sure, on the advice of wild swimmer Laura Owen Sanderson, the best safeguard against poisoning your gut is to down a can of Coca-Cola the moment you are back on the

bank. Many open-water swimmers swear that the phosphoric acid in Coke will kill any bacteria in your stomach (which is a fine reason never to touch the stuff, except medicinally). Although the science has not yet been robustly tested, it may be worth taking heed of open swimmers' experience and bringing a can with you for a long swim.

Wild Water Is Dangerous

Wild water *is* dangerous. The currents in our rivers can be exhaustingly strong, and the cold can be so shocking that it can turn your limbs into heavy weights, increasing the risk of sinking. Hypothermia can be deadly. But wild swimming is not the cause of the dangers in wild water, but rather the antidote. Most people who drown in England do so not by deliberately entering the water, but by falling in by accident. They are overcome by shock, and fear of an environment about which they have no experience.

Wild swimming should be a gentle immersion. Long before a solo swimmer attempts long distances along the course of a river, they will have built up their strength, experience and knowledge of the waterway through incremental advances. They will have gone first with parents or grandparents, then with friends as teenagers, then with groups, and often still swim with support vessels. To know the run of a river is to know its riverbed, its banks, where to get in and where to get out. It is to know the ecology of the area, and also, through experience and observation, the ways in which water is dangerous.

People don't drown in weirs because the water is thundering so heavily on their heads, but for the exact opposite reason: the water in a plunge pool is so aerated (full of bubbles) that it becomes lighter, not dense enough to hold a human body, no matter how hard they kick. The trick of escaping a weir alive is to grab a deep breath, let yourself sink, allow your body to be pushed out by the flow and kick to the surface when you are free of the morass. People's lives have been saved by knowing this, and lost by not knowing.

Landowners Are Liable

Unfortunately for them, land-owners *are* liable. But not to the extent that is commonly believed. Many landowners operate under the assumption that if an accident occurs in the river or reservoir they own, that the law will hold them personally responsible. This is unlikely, as the Outdoor Swimming Society says. Under civil case law and health-and-safety legislation, landowners are not liable as long as they have done an assessment to see if there are any unusual risks that cannot be seen and as long as they have taken steps to mitigate or warn about these. Someone who chooses to enter the water willingly accepts the risks that are obvious and usual in undertaking this activity and cannot succeed in a claim against the landowner if they suffer injury as a result.

Jean Perraton's book *Swimming Against the Stream* contains an excellent account of how this belief about landowners' liability came about, and how health-and-safety regulations introduced in the 1970s have been misread to make it much easier for a landowner to erect 'No Swimming' signs on their property than signs that inform and warn swimmers of potential risks. It is true that landowners use liability as an excuse to banish the public from their rivers, but it is the misty world of misinterpretation around river law that is the real culprit for our exclusion. Perraton's book dispels the myth of the evil landowner, and casts a light on the government's duty to make landowners and the public better informed.

WON IN WATER

The argument of greater public access rights to nature, and the eventual extension of a right to roam through green and blue space across England, will be won in water. Our exclusion from rivers is both too extreme in scale (97 per cent is ridiculous) and insupportable in logic to be tenable. Water is just too good for us, and exercising in water is just too popular for it to be banned by English law.

The popularity of our waterways has increased exponentially over lockdown. The Canal & River Trust, the Outdoor Swimming Society and the Angling Trust have all reported a surge in interest. British Canoeing has seen a 40 per cent rise in members since last year, with 19,000 people signing up in the first three months of lockdown. Red Paddle Co., a paddleboard retailer, have reported an unprecedented 300 per cent rise in sales and enquiries, making 2020 its busiest year and leaving stores short of stock. With this increase in activity on our rivers has come an increased awareness of the restrictions erected around them, from barbed wire strewn across the channels to the sudden interruption of a sunny-day paddle by a river bailiff or fisherman. Suddenly, rivers are being remembered, and so too is the great injustice of being evicted from them.

Until our access rights to blue space are secured, while the government is resolutely pretending that people don't swim outside, we swim in our rivers, reservoirs and lakes with no official guidance or advice. So it falls to another non-governmental organisation, the Outdoor Swimming Society, to spell out the guidelines for access to England's beautiful blue space in a way that is safe for both swimmers and the habitat itself. The Outdoor Swimmer's Code contains the same logic and sensitivity to people and the environment as the Scottish Outdoor Access Code. Under the headings 'Looking After the Environment', 'Consideration for Other People' and 'Swimming Safely and Responsibly', it spells out the specific philosophy of commoning – that ancient code of reciprocity, care and sustainability. Not only this, by teaching the rules of engagement, they also encourage a deeper knowledge of the habitat.

The Outdoor Swimming Society's website (outdoorswimmingsociety.com) goes into much more granular detail. There are blogs describing how to be aware of the needs of, and minimise our effects on, the habitats and species that thrive in our rivers and lakes. There is clear guidance on how to avoid eroding water margins, on whether swimming in nature reserves or SSSIs is acceptable, on the different effects of seasonality (fish spawning, insect breeding, etc.) and specific advice relating to amphibians, invertebrates, birds and fish. Not only does this advice safeguard the ecology of wild water, it teaches us about its intricacies. Swimming is a way of learning.

TAKE ACTION FOR ACCESS

Check out the advice for wild swimming on the Outdoor Swimming Society's website (outdoorswimmingsociety.com).

While you're at it, join in with their efforts to push for better access to our water by signing up to the Inland Access Group (outdoorswimmingsociety.com/access-all-areas).

Join the British Canoeing Association: a membership fee of £45 per year gives you the licence to paddle on 3 per cent of waterways that we have access to, but also contributes to supporting the work that waterway authorities carry out to maintain and protect managed waterways. Whether you're a member or not, you can sign up to take part in their excellent 'Clear Access, Clear Waters' campaign (clearaccessclearwaters. org.uk), which promotes greater access to our blue waters through actively improving their ecology.

FORAGING

Foraging is perhaps the best illustration of our ideal relationship with the natural world. Not only does it encourage a truly visceral experience of nature (eating it), but in doing so, it encourages exploration, education, attentiveness to the local specifics of fauna and seasonal fluctuations and – perhaps most vital in these post-industrialist times of exploitation – moderation.

The four Fs – fruits, flowers, fungi and foliage – are the substance of foraging, and the gathering of all of these is perfectly legal in England. However, all wild plants are protected under the Wildlife and Countryside

Act (1981), meaning it is illegal to dig up or remove a plant (including algae, lichens and fungi) from the land on which it is growing without permission from the landowner or occupier. From the act: 'If any person ... not being an authorised person, intentionally uproots any wild plant not included in that Schedule, he shall be guilty of an offence.' This makes gathering of roots such as dandelion or burdock illegal unless you have express permission to do so.

However, it is a lesser known clause in the Theft Act 1968 that makes foraging parts of a plant or fungus perfectly legal. Section 4 (3) states:

> **A person who picks mushrooms growing wild on any land,
> or who picks flowers, fruit or foliage from a plant growing wild
> on any land, does not (although not in possession of the land)
> steal what he picks, unless he does it for reward or for sale or
> other commercial purpose.**

So, if you're not foraging for your haute cuisine restaurant or looking to sell herbal tinctures, it is perfectly legal for you to pick wild flowers on private land. The only wrong you will be committing is trespass, and you cannot be arrested, at least on the first go, for that. What's more, a landowner who confronts you while you are trespassing on his or her land is unable to confiscate the contents of your basket, as they now belong to you – a nice touch.

You are allowed to forage along rights of way, and also in national parks, where some actively encourage foraging. You are also allowed to forage in SSSIs, as long as you don't damage the plant. In this instance, the burden of proof is on the local authority, who have to prove damage. However, mad as it might seem, the areas of land designated under the CRoW Act for public access carry specific prohibitions on foraging. Section 2 (1) 'does not entitle a person to be on any land if, in or on that land, he intentionally removes, damages or destroys any plant, shrub, tree or root or any part of a plant, shrub, tree or root'. The one type of land dedicated to bringing the public closer to nature is the very land that prohibits foraging. This must be changed.

Until then, again because the Countryside Code makes no reference to it at all, the Woodland Trust's guide to safe and sustainable foraging is provided overleaf (although point two might not be so relevant).

SUSTAINABLE FORAGING

Minimise damage

Take no more than you plan to consume. Stick to paths and take care not to trample down or damage areas you are collecting from. Uprooting plants is harmful, so pick leaves or berries with care, in moderation and avoid damaging plant roots.

Seek permission

On our sites, we do not allow foraging for commercial purposes, only for personal use. On some of our sites we prefer you not to forage, even for small amounts of fungi or other species. This is on sites that are important for conservation, are habitats for rare or vulnerable species or where there are problems with over-picking. These sites can be identified through signage on site, but please always check before setting off.

Know what you're picking

Never consume a wild plant or fungus unless you are absolutely certain of its identification. It could be rare and protected, inedible or even deadly poisonous. Use reference books to identify them. Fungi can be notoriously difficult to identify, so if you're unsure it's best to leave alone.

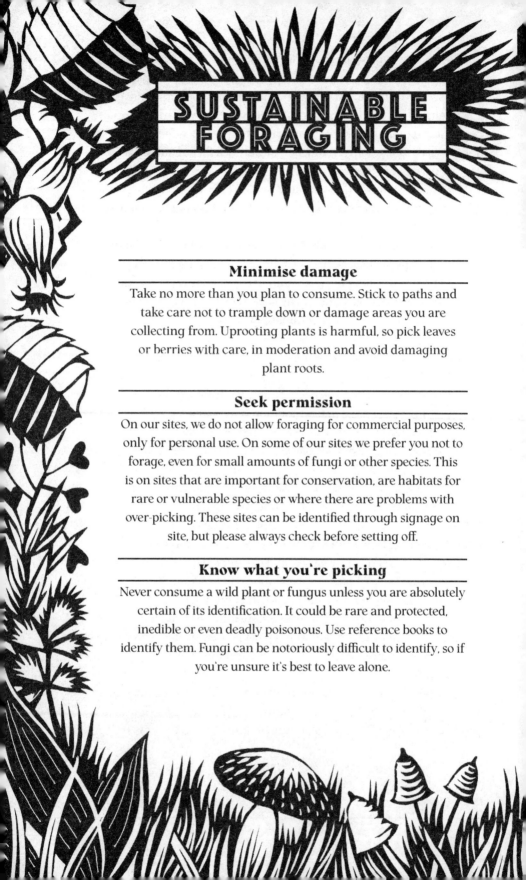

Only collect from plentiful populations

Only collect flowers, leaves, fruits and seeds where they are in abundance. For fungi, only take mushrooms that have opened their caps (so are likely to have dropped their spores). Do not collect small 'button' mushrooms.

Leave plenty behind

Wild food is vital for the survival of the UK's wildlife. Forage carefully to ensure there is enough left for birds and species to consume now and to ensure plants and fungi can regenerate and reproduce. You may not be the only person foraging, and plants and fungi need to produce seeds and spores to grow into the next generation.

Do not collect rare species

Only take plants and fungi when you are certain you know what they are. Take a good field guide to confirm species in the field and avoid confusion. Some species are protected by law, so know what not to collect. Ancient woods, in particular, can contain many rare species so take special care. If you're not sure, it's best to leave it alone.

Maria Fernandez Garcia

Founder of Healing Weeds

It took me ages to open my eyes to the sea of green on the roadside verge. I was an educator for children for much of my adult life, a support worker for children with additional needs. With a bit of hindsight, I now see that I had this constant urge to get them outside, building bat boxes and exploring the woods; I knew that there was something important out there for them, and for me. So I went on a bushcraft training course and taught in a few camps. Then I moved to Bristol and ended up teaching about sixty kids every couple of days. Most of the kids were from cities and started the courses not wanting to kneel in the mud. But seeing them just twenty minutes later, crawling around, mud on their faces, gave me joy. When you live in a box, the countryside feels alien, so they were uncertain of themselves – but they became comfortable in it so quickly.

Then I found herbal medicine. The thing that got me was that I didn't realise how powerful it was, its ability to help people with small and large ailments and illnesses. I started researching, and thought, wow, these things I'm learning about are all there on a basic walk. Medicines that you're prescribed from a pharmacy seem so far away, so unknowable, but all these powerful medicines are literally here, in the park in Bristol, on a walk in the country. There's no separation between myself and my healing.

I quit my job and set up my own business teaching foraging. I wanted to pass on my feeling that foraging isn't just about extracting a bit of nature for yourself. By learning about nettles, for example, you start noticing them more, where they grow well, how tall they are, if they need water, what their life cycle is, and then you start seeing the spaces in between them and wondering what other plants there are. You start to feel a familiarity with what's in front of you, even if you've never been there before.

Foraging leads you into nature. And close-up, you get to see its intricacies; you notice little things. We give prominence to people in this world, and actually there's loads of other things that are living, breathing, doing stuff all around us. I was collecting Alexander seeds just the other day, pod by pod, and lifted one up to find a bee asleep on the underside. On that same walk, I saw a patch of nettles with their leaves curling. I wondered why they were curled, lifted one up, to find an insect nymph tucked in the curve. Foraging takes you into the detail, the spaces in between, lets you see the little things nesting and feeding, living.

It's about slowness. For me, foraging goes hand in hand with being careful and considerate, and that means you have to be slower, to think about what you're doing. It changes the pace of your walk, because even if you're walking, your mind can be really quick, just thinking about one thing or another. Foraging gives you a focus, it gives you an attentiveness that is mindful or meditative. And the slower you are, the more considerate you become. If you're collecting rose petals, for example, and you're plucking each petal rather than taking the whole head, that head will become a rosehip, which provides food for other animals. You begin to think more purposefully about those things.

My basket is never full. You see all these images of foraging in Sunday magazine supplements, and they've all got these huge, overbrimming baskets, to make it seem luscious. I always notice that. I come back with just enough, sometimes less. I'm too distracted by nature to fill up that basket. There's a risk that people will think foraging is all about harvesting free food, that it encourages a selfish attitude. But it's not that. It's not just about us; it's about all of us, human and non-human.

NATURE JOURNALLING

The lost art of nature journalling is both the foundation of modern science and a fun, low-cost thing to do while out and about. The art of recording nature, in images and words, paying close attention to detail, is a vital practice in science and is still taught at some universities. But even if you're not doing field studies for laboratory work, there is still a great deal to be gained from not just bringing a sketchbook with you, but following the rigours of the nature journal.

Drawing and painting are excellent ways to increase one's mindfulness in nature. But more than this, by pausing for a while in nature, the rest of the world

relaxes with your stillness. When you are sat drawing, animals relax out of their state of alert – birdsong changes, mammals come out of hiding, you see the world as it is without human intervention.

Closely observing detail helps you learn the differences between species, allowing you to recognise indicators. Having spent time putting them onto

paper, this learning becomes less cerebral, less academic and more intuitive. To collect each drawing and excerpt together in one notebook results in a beautiful, unique object in and of itself. Your nature journal will become a unique record of your experience, a token of your love and learning of nature and a fingerprint of your relationship to the wild. And all you need is a notebook and pen.

PERFORM RITUALS

These days, traditional British Wicca is revered the world over. It is a fairly recent reassembling of old pagan traditions, hermetic and esoteric cultures, reimagined into rituals for the modern day. First introduced to the public in 1954 by retired civil servant Gerald Gardner, it is today officially recognised as a modern pagan religion, with almost 70,000 people identifying as pagan or Wiccan in the 2011 UK census. While this is not a huge proportion of our population, it is worth remembering that it is exactly double the number of people who own half of England.

Wicca is an open, non-hierarchical religion, meaning you can dip your toe into it without having to fully immerse yourself in the lifestyle. The occult side of it, the Aleister Crowleyisms, sex magick and Satan worship is there if you want it (and almost universally misinterpreted), but on the fringes it is a simple, subtle structure of symbols and practices that allow people to ritualise their relationship with nature and society, to think about their past, present and future.

If there are any rules in Wicca, they can be found in the basic Wiccan Rede, an eight-word mantra that is both a moral outlook on the world and the pithiest summary you'll ever find in all the right-to-roam codes in Europe: 'An it harm none, do what thou wilt'. In other words, do what you want to, as long as it doesn't harm anything else. What is so appealing about the Wiccan Rede is that it foregrounds the issue of morality in our relationship with nature. It offers a more profound rationale for having a gentle presence in nature that goes deeper than respecting property rights, national legislation or the industrial mechanics of the countryside, and asks instead for you to consider your moral duties to society and nature.

On top of that, Wicca offers something else to do in nature. It takes us back to another lost connection, another severance of enclosure, that connection we feel to the dead, the living and those to come. It is hard enough to talk to loved ones about tragedy or death or illness, and harder still to do it in the busy noise of our urbanised lives. People don't just enter nature for their love of it, or for their mental and physical health, but also because it offers us space, vast vistas of natural growth, that allow our memories and words to flow. Take another esoteric practice: Tarot. You can either believe that Tarot cards offer us a direct link to the metaphysical world, or that they simply reframe our reality in a way that we can think about it differently. Wicca allows for the same breadth of interpretation: you can either believe in its power to connect us with an underlying truth, or you can see it simply as another way of looking at life. Wicca offers us a way of talking, or thinking, about those we love in a way that celebrates our connection to the passing life of the world around us. This aspect of our relationship with nature is never mentioned in parliamentary discussions on the right to roam, you'll not find it on the Ramblers' website, but it is a crucial element to being alive that has been severed from the general public by barbed wire. Wicca simply offers you rituals and practices to lead you back into this rich heritage of natural connection, a stile over the fences erected by private property.

Wicca is also notable for its strong feminist credentials. It is no accident that Wicca and covens are popular with women, because, as anthropologist Susan Greenwood has said of Wicca rituals, they are 'a form of resistance to mainstream culture ... a healing space away from the ills of the wider culture' and one in which female practitioners can 'redefine and empower themselves'. Nature is a place for women to go outside of the male gaze, because very simply, if it is wild and remote enough, there aren't many men around.

There are any number of books and websites dedicated to the diverse and multifarious strands of Wicca. If you fancy trying something new with friends, if you have something you'd like to talk about, and haven't found the moment, or right place, find one you like the look of, find a spell or a ritual and take it out into nature with you. And don't stop for the fences.

SAWALDEOR

This word comes from the Old English words *sawal* ('soul') and *deor* ('animal'). Your soul or 'spirit' animal is very simply the creature you feel most kinship towards. But, like Philip Pullman's daemons in *His Dark Materials*, there are harmonies we find in the spirit of certain animals that resonate with our own selves – our souls, our personality types, our unique fascinations. And why not celebrate that? For some, the idea of a spirit animal is fanciful hippy piffle; for others, it is a dangerous appropriation of indigenous cultures, casually cherry-picking values from oppressed cultures and using them as memes. But it could be a useful tool for protecting our fauna.

Though the concept of a magical connection between human and animal is found in many animist cultures, it is most commonly associated with Native American tribes. The insult of appropriation is more complex in this particular instance, largely because there is no such term as 'spirit animal' actually found in any historical Native American language. Certain tribes did practice a philosophy of animal guides, of which several could visit you in a lifetime, but the magical connection between the human and non-human is celebrated in cultures across the world.

Before enclosure, and before the systemic oppression of the people of the commons, English folk tradition had its own concept of sawaldeor: the familiar. Familiar spirits were usually small, local animals, such as cats, dogs, birds, frogs and hares, but there were occasional instances of butterflies, wasps and farmyard animals. These familiars were sometimes visible, sometimes not, and they helped the witches of England perform their magic.

There is a modern-day use for the concept of sawaldeor. On a basic level, assigning yourself a spirit animal is a great portal into the wonder of the natural world. It can turn a simple walk into a magical event – spying the hare through the hedges, glimpsing the redstart flashing through the trees. Whether your spirit animal is a wood pigeon, which you may well spot twenty or thirty times on a walk, or a polecat, which you might be lucky enough to see once or twice in your life, assigning yourself a spirit animal gives a new magic to a walk and takes you to different places in the hope of seeing them.

To single out one animal is not to disregard the others, it is to take personal responsibility for the well-being of its species. By picking an animal and learning about its life, its folklore and its habitats, we can learn about its wider context. Learning about animals is the most effective way we can love them. Learn about the animal, learn where it lives, how it lives, what its threats are, how it's doing during the sixth largest mass extinction on earth. Then find the organisation that exists to defend it, join it and help them out. To find a spirit animal is to focus your efforts on one species, to make its survival and thriving your personal cause.

All of the guest writers in this book are illustrated as their sawaldeor. And the diversity of animals represented shows how different we all are, how nature speaks to us all in idiosyncratic, specific terms. If we all protected the parts we loved, the diversity of human beings would ensure the diversity of nature could thrive. Every species should have its advocates. Even the wasps and hornets. Even the ticks.

OI!

'Everyone can go out there,
right now, and become a defender
of your local river's rights, and
if you are prepared to break the
law of trespass that stops you,
you can change that law and
protect your river.'

PAUL POWESLAND,
FOUNDER OF LAWYERS FOR NATURE

In 1932, about four hundred kids walked up a hill. They strayed off the designated path by a couple of hundred metres, and their act was considered so heinous that a group of men employed by the Duke of Devonshire beat them with sticks. Later, six of the kids that organised the walk were imprisoned.

At the time, popular reaction to the Kinder Trespass was one of almost universal outrage, and yet today, the same organisations – from the press to the ramblers' charities and even landowners – treat it with a bizarre reverence, celebrating it in a way that represents a 180-degree U-turn from their initial reaction. History can make hypocrites of us all.

In the context of the fight for greater access to nature, the Kinder Trespass was in fact a minor event. Compare it to the Winter Hill Trespass of 1896, which brought 10,000 local Boltonians together, or the thousands of people who met at Winnats Pass a week after Kinder, you begin to wonder what made the Kinder Trespass lodge so firmly in the national memory. In one respect, these trespasses serve as a testament to just how long social change takes; the Kinder Trespass didn't achieve its goal (open access on the moors) until two decades after the fact, while the participants of the Winter Hill Trespass were all dead before the right of way blocked a century before was officially reopened in 1996. But perhaps Kinder's greatest worth today is as a prism through which to see how reaction to social progress mutates over time. Challenging the most ingrained orthodoxies of our society results in the largest levels of outrage, but several decades later, when the point has resolutely been proven, those that were cast as villains are now celebrated as national heroes.

Over the course of ninety years, the semiotics of the Kinder Trespass have changed: what was first punk graffiti daubed on the walls of the establishment is now a sepia-toned photograph hung on the corridors inside the establishment. On the one hand this is effective, because the notion of public access has become further cemented into the architecture of our society. The problem, however, is that we now venerate the very minor ground it gained, without considering the future and questioning what comes next. We need to remember that the Kinder Trespass was not the act of national heroes but normal, regular people who wanted access to nature. And there is still so much more ground to be gained.

Trespass is a simple expression of freedom. By taking a step over a line that has no moral justification, it is an act of defiance against the unfair and exclusive system that created that line. But on its own, it is not going to change that system. Similarly, by taking a dip in a river or a stroll in some woodland, you will have improved your day and improved your health, but you will not have improved the lives of others who have been so excluded from nature that even the option to visit has been forgotten under years of segregation. This book is not simply an encouragement to trespass more but a direct plea for your help to change an unfair, elitist system that for a thousand years has benefited the few at the expense of the many. And you can do it by swimming, walking, climbing, paddling, drawing, writing and snoozing – by trespassing.

DIRECT ACTION

The main difference between a simple trespass and direct action is spectacle. Direct action elevates a simple act into a protest by playing to an audience. It designs the action with the audience in mind; it plays into the media template to generate a story, in order that the act becomes more than itself: an evocative expression of the problem it seeks to solve.

The best explanation of direct action are the six steps published by the Martin Luther King, Jr., Research and Education Institute, based in Stanford University in California. The guidelines are adapted from an essay written by Martin Luther King, Jr., called 'Letter from a Birmingham Jail' and listed overleaf.

It doesn't take much to turn a trespass into a spectacle. Simply crossing over a barbed-wire fence triggers enough 'creative tension' for a spectacle. There is no need for banners (though they work), no need for speeches or a megaphone (though they also work). The most dramatic thing to do on land you don't have rights to is exactly what you would do if you did. To repeat the words of David Graeber from the start of this book, 'The principle of direct action is the defiant insistence on acting as if one is already free.' If we were allowed to swim in our nation's rivers, and picnic on the banks, and doze in a glade of a gorgeous woodland, there's very little chance we would bellow through a megaphone as we did it. There is just one simple step you have to take to progress a simple trespass into a direct action: make it public.

NON-VIOLENT DIRECT ACTION

Step One: Information Gathering

Identify the issues in your community and/or school in need of positive change. To understand the issue, problem or injustice facing a person, community, or institution, you must increase your understanding of the problem. Your investigation should include all sides of the issue and may include formal research and listening to the experiences of others.

Step Two: Educating Others

It is essential to inform others, including your opposition, about your issue. In order to cause change, the people in the community must be aware of the issue and understand its impact. By educating others you will minimise misunderstanding and gain support and allies.

Step Three: Personal Commitment

Check and affirm your faith in the philosophy and methods of non-violence. Causing change requires dedication and long hours of work. Meet with others regularly to stay focused on your goal. Prepare yourself to accept sacrifices, if necessary, in your work for justice.

Step Four: Negotiations

Using grace, humour and intelligence, confront the individuals who need to participate in this change. Discuss a plan for addressing and resolving these injustices. Look for what is positive in every action and statement the opposition makes. Do not seek to humiliate the opponent but call forth the good in the opponent. Look for ways in which the opponent can become an ally.

Step Five: Direct Action

These are actions taken to convince others to work with you in resolving the injustices. Direct action imposes a 'creative tension' into the conflict. Direct action is most effective when it illustrates the injustice it seeks to correct. There are hundreds of direct action, including: boycotts, marches and rallies, letter-writing and petition campaigns, political action and voting, public art and performance.

Step Six: Reconciliation

Non-violence seeks friendship and understanding. Non-violence does not seek to defeat the opponent. Non-violence is directed against evil systems, oppressive policies and unjust acts, not against persons.

"WE WHO ENGAGE IN NON VIOLENT DIRECT ACTION ARE NOT THE CREATORS OF TENSION. WE MERELY BRING TO THE SURFACE HIDDEN TENSION THAT IS ALREADY ALIVE."

- DR MARTIN LUTHER KING JR

Benny Rothman leading the Kinder Trespsass, 1932

HOW TO **REALLY** TAKE ACTION FOR ACCESS

The best way to get things done is to *actually* do them. If any of the ideas of this book resonate with you, then take action and do them. Trespass is an incredibly effective means of protest for greater public access: it worked for the National Parks Act, it worked for the CRoW Act and if enough of us actually go out to do it, it will work again today for the right to roam.

The tactic of the mass trespass is necessarily rare; it takes far too much organising to become a regular, consistent event. But there are other ways to make it 'mass'. Instead of a thousand people coming together on one site, why not have a hundred groups of ten people trespassing their own local area on one day, or have a consistent stream of trespasses, researched and collected together under one roof. Local newspapers are interested in local events and will be inclined to report on a trespass on an area of local importance. And if these trespasses are co-ordinated, then all of a sudden national press outlets will become more interested. This model allows the issue of greater public access to be expressed both in local and national terms, which is a perfect illustration of the dynamic at the heart of the Right to Roam campaign – we are for local access on a national level.

SET UP A RIGHT-TO-ROAM GROUP

By trespassing on your own, or with a group of friends, each direct action becomes an easy, enjoyable event, with none of the relentless Zoom meetings and bureaucracy necessary to stage a mass trespass. But all over England there are book groups, rambling groups, swimming groups, climbing clubs, botany clubs and many more special-interest groups that meet socially to share their enthusiasm. So why not combine the lot, and set up a right-to-roam group. Meet up when you can, not only to plan trespasses, but to share thoughts and insights, pore over ancient maps and discuss books. Of course, you don't always have to trespass together, but a centralised group can allow fellow trespassers to share knowledge and experience, and to plan larger trespasses in the future.

Start small. Suggest a group meeting with some like-minded friends, plan the trespass, then go for a walk in the woods or a swim in the river. Researching and planning a trespass is no different from planning a walk or swim with your friends and is a great way of learning about the historical context of the land you live in. Let the group grow in its own time, and if it feels right, make active efforts to encourage people from outside your social circle, with particular emphasis on those groups that are so marginalised from the countryside that a walk in the woods with friends seems alien to them. While doing so, bear in mind that a trespass not only feels more dangerous for a member of those marginalised groups, but in very real terms can carry much more serious implications. Discuss how you can work together to safeguard more vulnerable members of your group, how to shield them from the bias that leaves them more exposed to the mechanics of the state.

TRESPASSERSCOMPANION.ORG

Our website is the companion to the companion. It is here to help you. Aside from the references that support this book, you will find various posters, memes and template press releases that you can download to help share the message. But, crucially, the website also contains one central interactive element that allows you to publish your trespass. In so doing you will be able to transform a simple swim, kayak, climb or walk into direct action, a statement that supports the right to roam for the whole country. You will be able to contribute your personal experience to a wider movement. Treat it as an individual toolkit for collective action.

The website has a form to fill in that allows you to upload photos of your trespass and add text describing why you chose this destination and how it fits into the general picture of our exclusion from the countryside. Fill in the context of the place, the history of the land, when was it enclosed, what is it used for now, how many people could benefit from access, but also describe your own connection to the land, why it is important to you. Design your trespass around the communication of a message. Use your photos and text to make a point and try to make that point as clear as possible. Try to theme your trespass in line with the ideals of the campaign, as outlined in this book, and think creatively about how best to represent them on the ground. For example, the theme of caring for nature could translate into a trespass with an expert botanist, a group sketching trip or a trespass to gather water-pollution samples. All of these ideas demonstrate a love of nature that contradicts the notion that the public are a threat to the countryside. Or if you choose to highlight the theme of how essential nature is to our well-being, then simply tell us where you went and how it felt to be there. How nature makes you feel might not be relevant to the law or given credence by politicians and landowners, but it is hugely significant to the rest of us.

Take lots of beautiful photos, close-ups of the flora and fauna you discover, big sweeping landscapes of the land or water you trespassed, and if you want, include an in-situ photo of our 'Everybody Welcome' sign, which can be downloaded from the website. Print off the sign, take some tape and stick it over the 'Private' signs. We need to change the semiotics of the countryside, from a foreboding place of exclusion to a welcoming place that encourages diversity and exploration.

Each trespass will be a small direct action against the behemoth orthodoxy that keeps us out of nature, but when collected together, each will work with the other to demonstrate the public's appetite for natural connection and our willingness to change the law by overstepping its boundaries.

A NOTE ON FUN

On 16 October 2019, *ITV* aired a live interview between Piers Morgan, Susanna Reid and Mr Broccoli on *Good Morning Britain*. Mr Broccoli was representing Extinction Rebellion, demanding that Britain move to a plant-based diet, and was doing so dressed in mirrored aviators, a face painted broccoli green and a big, fluffy, woollen broccoli hat.

As Piers himself noted, the broccoli get-up was the element that got him on telly in the first place. But what followed was an excruciating seven-minute battle between two systems: one, the Apollonian Piers and Susanna, in formal attire, representing the serious business of the nation; second, the Dionysian Mr Broccoli, puckish, satirical, refusing to accept the po-faced reverence that accompanies matters of state importance. The orthodoxy demands you take it seriously and needs you to believe that satire, humour and silliness are superfluous fripperies.

But they are much more than that. Earlier on in the year, Piers had inter-viewed another Extinction Rebellion activist, and again attacked them for having fun. He claimed that the dancing of activists in the streets was undermining their cause. Opponents of a cause often feign a deep concern for the cause itself, framing their attack in a way that suggests they are only trying to offer solutions. This is the very essence of paternalism, and bless Mr Broccoli and his fellow activists for remaining composed under such a shower of condescension.

But what's going on here has been thought out. Dancing and singing have been used as tactics among activists since time immemorial. Not only do dancing and singing bind a group together, generating solidarity, they also solve two problems that can threaten most protests: boredom and cold. Many protests involve sitting around for long periods of time, which can lead to seriously cold bums and quietly bored participants. Singing and dancing cures this, giving people something to do communally. It helps people enjoy themselves, which means they are more likely to stay and to come back again. Fun makes protest sustainable.

The same dynamic exists in the countryside. Just because the architecture of exclusion demands that we take it seriously does not mean we have to. Just because razor wire can be lethal and walls impose an austere authority upon the countryside does not mean our actions have to follow suit. To really trespass the walls that divide us from nature, we have to act as if they weren't there in the first place, as if the countryside welcomed our presence, as if the joy we feel in nature wasn't forbidden. Make your group meetings fun, make your trespasses joyful, and then make them public. Change will follow.

MAKE ART

In 2019, the Sheffield Tree Campaign asked writer Rob Macfarlane to compose a poem to aid their efforts to stop the council chopping down 17,500 of their street trees. He wrote 'Heartwood', a poem that evokes the universe of each tree, 'a city of butterflies, a country of creatures', and conjures a memory of what trees have always been in our culture: gods that watch over the scurrying of humans with a time-drawn wisdom.

The poem was designed into a laser-cut medallion by the illustrator Jackie Morris, which was hung from trees destined for the council chop. It was also illustrated as a poster so people could purchase it and hang it on the walls of their house or download the PDF from a website and print it out. This final touch allowed people to disseminate the message themselves, and the poster found its way into the advert hoardings of local bus-stop shelters, courtesy of local subvertisers.

Macfarlane called his poem a 'charm against harm', a spell to protect the trees and those that protect them. But what good is a poem to stand up to PFI contracts and arborists armed with chainsaws? What followed was a lesson in magic. Macfarlane's cultural capital, his talent and his many hundreds of thousands of followers on social media made sure that this local campaign hit the national and international spotlight. But the poem did more than that. Because Macfarlane had waived his copyright on the piece, the campaigners were able to produce high-quality prints of the poster, at nothing but cost, and sell them to raise money for the campaign. The poem raised enough money to pay for the legal costs of the tree defenders who, it later turned out, had been illegally removed by the police. By paying for their court costs, the poem literally kept the protestors out of jail. Words forged inside a poet's head, painted in ink by an illustrator, were dissolving the walls of a prison, permeating the power of a system, being used to keep people free. Macfarlane was right: this really was a charm against harm.

As it turned out, the poem sold so well that, long after the protestors had been acquitted, there was a surplus in the pot, which was donated to Lawyers for Nature, another grassroots organisation set up to evolve environmental law, to give trees and rivers legal rights. And again, because no fees were attached to the poem, it flew over national boundaries and has been used in various campaigns across the world, including the Fairy

Rob Macfarlane's 'Heartwood' poem, written for the Sheffield Tree Campaign

Creek blockade on Vancouver Island, Canada, and (translated into Telugu) by protesters in Hyderabad, India, to resit the felling of 300 banyans.

But amid all these effects of Macfarlane's poem, it was the words themselves that provided the most crucial addition to the battle to save Sheffield's trees. His words manifested a sentiment, an emotional response to the tree-felling that had been absent in the decision-making process between the council and the PFI contractors and police and private security firms hired to evict the tree defenders. The processes that exclude us from nature are cold, soulless mechanics that seek to override our emotional connection to nature, yet art, the charismatic expression of the soul, rebalances the scales and reminds us what these debates are really about.

So, yes, art can change the world we live in. And the Right to Roam movement needs your art. This campaign is for everyone, so whether you like making films or sculptures, whether you write poetry or short stories, whether you paint, dance, sing, draw or frottage, we'd like you to dedicate your talents to the Right to Roam movement. There is a list of statistics further on in this chapter that might help you as a springboard for inspiration.

You don't have to be a master magician like Rob Macfarlane or Jackie Morris to create work that ignites passions and summons the emotion of our connection to nature. The very act of making art is in itself an indication of how much we love nature, and belies the old cliché that we, the public, don't give a damn. So if you like drawing and painting but aren't confident enough to post your works online, then why not organise a trespass trip with like-minded friends, and go sketching out in the open air. Remember, with sketching, the image you make is the least important part – what really counts is the process, that deep observation of nature, that meditative state of being ensconced in a landscape, and responding to it. Nothing undermines the accusation that trespassers are vandals better than a gentle watercolour expedition over the wall of an estate.

SING A SONG

Singing is solidarity. To sing together is to create a vibration in our chests that binds us together in a shared physical, emotional and even neurological state. To sing an old song binds you to the other people who have sung that song, who will sing that song; it strengthens the lineage between people across time.

On our trespasses, we are not trying to avoid getting caught. We are not sneaking around the hedgerows, skulking through the laurel; we are not ashamed of our actions. Instead, if we are living as if we are free already, we will do our best to feel at ease in nature and there is nothing that makes you feel more at ease than belting out an old song. We will sing our chests full of the new vibrations, that new feeling of belonging to the countryside.

There are already a number of great English folk songs about our common rights to land. Check out a couple of recent albums to hear some of the best ones. *Stand Up Now*, released in 2021 by the Landworkers' Alliance, is a collection of new and old folk songs played by land workers, land activists and professional musicians. The album contains songs such as 'The Cutty Wren', thought to have been written as early as the fourteenth century, during the Peasants' Revolt, and 'The World Turned Upside Down', a song written in 1975 about the Diggers' occupation of St George's Hill in 1649. Its words link us to a time when the notion of reciprocal rights and responsibilities to the land were much better understood, and where the injustice at having them taken away was felt more keenly than it is today:

> **You poor take courage.**
> **You rich take care.**
> **This earth was made a common treasury**
> **For everyone to share.**

Even more recent is the eponymous album from Three Acres and a Cow, a travelling show of musicians, social historians and storytellers, which tells the forgotten land struggles of British radical history through folk song and story. Released in spring 2022, it features songs from as far back as the 1700s and it includes perhaps our most famous song about trespassing, 'The Manchester Rambler'. Folk singer Ewan MacColl, or James Henry Miller as he was then called, was seventeen when he joined the Kinder Trespass, and the solidarity he experienced during that direct action caused him to compose a song that has been sung by countless ramblers ever since.

But while singing songs of the past, we must create new songs for a new movement. Luckily, gruff-voiced balladeer Mr Beans on Toast, the Leonard Cohen of Kent, has stepped up and written a song for us all to sing. Titled

'The Commons', he's put his money where his mouth is and dedicated the song to the Creative Commons, which means you can sing it, use it or even remix it for free, without paying royalties. Just like Macfarlane's 'Heartwood', this simple change in the song's status allows us to reprint the lyrics here free of charge, and gives the song a freedom of movement to roam where it will across the lines of privatisation. You can find a video of Beans on Toast performing song on the website (TrespassersCompanion.org) and listen to it on his most recent album, *Survival of the Friendliest*.

TAKE ACTION FOR ACCESS

Listen to the song, learn its lyrics, learn how to play it (like all good folk songs, it is, as Hank Williams put it, 'just three chords and the truth'). Sometime in the future, there might be a time and a place where we all have to sing it together.

Write your own trespass song, and don't limit yourself to folk. Anyone who has walked wearing headphones knows the English landscape can accommodate any genre of music, from Elgar to Iron Maiden, from Mumford and Sons to the Sons of Kemet.

THE COMMONS

Well. ...
If you don't take down this fence
I'll hop over it anyway
I've done some reading
And things don't have to be this way

You're worried I might climb the wall
and stumble across your family tree
I bet you there's some roots down there
You don't want me to see

Because your Ancestors they stole this land
Fenced it off in a power grab
And ripped it from beneath the feet
of the folks who used to dwell on it
Drilled it into the consciousness
For a couple of hundred years
And now its so ingrained
that no one even questions it

Who can go where? Who owns what?
And how much land have you got?

Because...
We're craving bird song And a lonley sunrise
An ancient tree
And wildflowers in the summertime
Swimming in the lake Sleeping beneath the stars
These simple things they are inherently ours
But when one man owns 15,000 acres
Well that doesn't sound fair
to the Common Folk of England

Class/Money/Power And land ownership
Who gets to decide whats in the local interest
This is more than just a fence
Around the countryside
By fencing off the commons they're fencing off our minds

And we're only given acess to a smidgen of our rivers
And we're going stir crazy in the towns and the cities
Knowing nature can fill that hole
We just need a
  RIGHT TO ROAM

We just want to walk the land
treat it like common ground
We want to feel at home and welcome in nature
Stop saying that the country's full
And hiding it behind a wall
Well anyone who crosses gets labeled a trespasser

Who can go where? Who owns what?
And how much land have you got?

Because...
We're craving bird song and a lonely sunrise
An ancient tree
And wildflowers in the summertime
Swimming in the lake sleeping beneath the stars
These simple things they are inherently ours
But when one man owns 50,000 acres
Well that doesn't sound fair
to the Common Folk of England

If you don't take down this fence
   We'll hop over it anyway
We come in numbers
And things don't have
to be this way.

Beans
x

Stat Pack

Here are a few salient statistics to help make the argument that we, the public, need greater access to nature. These stats are just the bare bones, the dry facts. It's up to you to go through them, find the ones that resonate and express them to people in your own way. If some of the stats tell a wider story of the situation in your local area, then tell that specific localised story first, and tie it in with the wider context. Do this in conversation or online, or design a trespass to illustrate the injustice of a particular stat, and then publish it on TrespassersCompanion.org.

92 per cent of English land is out of bounds to the public. Of this, only 6 per cent is built on. 56 per cent is given to agricultural production, livestock and growing crops.

---

97 per cent of rivers are out of bounds to the public.

There are roughly 117,000 miles of public footpath in England. As, on average, each path is two metres wide (the legal minimum requirement, which is rarely exceeded), this amounts to just 0.3 per cent of the landmass.

---

1 per cent of England's population owns 50 per cent of its land. On average, each of this 1 per cent owns 10,600 acres each, while 55 million English citizens own on average 0.07 acres.

One in eight families in England (3.3 million people) have no access to a garden. The figure ranges from 3 per cent of households in South Tyneside, to 40 per cent of homes in the London borough of Tower Hamlets.

Eleven million people in England live in areas categorised as having the lowest level of green space, with less than nine square metres of public green space per person, few gardens and 75 per cent of residents having to walk more than five minutes to find larger green areas.

Only 16.2 per cent of people in the UK have access to a wood of at least two hectares within 500 metres of their home. An additional 37 per cent of the population would have a local accessible wood if access rights were given to existing woods.

England's fourteen green belts cover nearly 13 per cent of England, significant not only because of their extent, but because with greater access rights, they could provide open-air recreation for 60 per cent of the population (30 million people) living in the urban areas within green belt boundaries.

Around 64 per cent of England's population lives within fifteen miles of a protected landscape, this leaves around 36 per cent of the population outside of the catchment. The results show that there are significant gaps, particularly the area between Leicester, Grantham, Stamford and Kettering. This area is the furthest distance from any protected landscape in England.

Of the 27 million people who live in the largest towns and cities, approximately 10.4 million are outside of the fifteen-mile catchment of national parks and AONBs. Shockingly, almost half of people in the most deprived areas of the country are outside of the catchment, so are less likely to reap the benefits of landscapes designated for the whole nation.

Visitors to national parks overwhelmingly rely on driving to get there, with 93 per cent of journeys made by car. But the majority of areas where less than half of all households own a car also fall outside of the accessible range of these landscapes. This means that most people who live furthest from England's most beautiful landscapes have to rely on public transport (which no longer exists) to reach them.

―――――――

Only 1 per cent of visitors to UK national parks are people of colour, and statistics from the outdoor sector paint a similar picture, with only around 1 per cent of summer mountain leaders and rock-climbing instructors in the UK coming from ethnic minorities.

―――――――

According to the data, more than two-fifths (42 per cent) of people from minority ethnic groups live in England's most green space–deprived neighbourhoods, compared with just one in five white people.

―――――――

In 2011, 13 per cent of the UK population (8.1 million people), identified themselves as Black, Asian or from a minority ethnic group. Yet a 2017 study by Natural England found that just 26.2 per cent of black people spent time in the countryside, compared with 44.2 per cent of white people. According to the study, LGBT people who were 'noticeably different' in small rural communities were more likely to be victims of hate crime.

―――――――

Although two-thirds (65 per cent) of adults reported that local green space had always been important to them, an additional one in five adults (19 per cent) said green space was more important to them now than before the Covid-19 crisis.

―――――――

In October 2020, 88 per cent of adults agreed that green spaces were good for their mental health and well-being, and 82 per cent said that 'being in nature makes me very happy'.

Thanks to Sam Siva of LION and righttoroam.org.uk for compiling these stats.

Paul Powesland

Barrister and co-founder of Lawyers for Nature

I remember once, as a teenager, my grandma was selling her house to developers, and there was this huge 500-year-old pollarded oak tree in the back of her garden that they were planning to cut down after the sale. I was only fourteen, but I figured out I could apply for a Tree Protection Order to save the tree. My family persuaded me not to on the strength that it would stop the sale of my granny's house. I still feel the pain of that tree being cut down.

That personal connection to nature has always been there, but it really deepened in my twenties. I had studied law at university, and was working as a barrister in London, when I went to a couple of festivals. I was there for hedonism, but what actually happened was that I felt this profound connection to the environment around me, a real spiritual awakening. I began going out into nature to wild camp and swim and also started planting trees, some in official schemes, some in guerrilla-gardening activism – in other words, illegally. When you plant trees, you realise how difficult it is to get the saplings to take, to root and thrive. And you think, Even if they survive, they are not going to grow into the size of the trees around me until long after I'm dead. I began to realise how necessary it is to protect what we have already. For a decade, none of my work as a barrister had any connection to my principles, but eventually, I realised I had to find a way to join the two sides of my life, to use my legal skills to protect nature.

In 2017, in the early days of the Sheffield tree campaign, where locals were just starting to organise themselves to get out onto the streets and stand between the trees they loved and the chainsaws that threatened to fell them, I got in touch to offer my services, and almost immediately got a message back saying, 'Oh thank god, we're getting arrested for standing under trees, even ones in our own gardens. We don't think it's lawful, but the police won't stop. We need a QC to write us advice for this coming Monday.' I wrote back to tell them: I'm not a QC, but I'll do my best. I wrote twenty pages of legal advice and sent it to them at midnight on Sunday. The advice said that the police had misread the letter of the law, and in fact were themselves acting unlawfully. The next day the police left and never came back.

That was a really crucial juncture for the Sheffield tree campaign and for my life; it was a real eye-opener to see what direct action could actually achieve. The amazing commitment of the people who stood around the trees and peacefully said no to the council's plans, that kind of thing really works. The council had every legal card in the pack, but what made the difference was that a small number of people said no, and in doing so, they were willing to go to jail to stand by what they believed in. They called the law's bluff. It is such a piece of alchemy, what happens when people stand up to the law.

If someone says, 'No, I disagree with your law and I'm not going to obey it,' there are actually very limited options for the law. They can put you in jail, they can take your stuff, and that's it. For some things, the law is willing to do that; if you kill someone, the law will put you in prison. But where your cause is clearly just, where you are acting peacefully, where a lot of people agree with your actions, where it is patently ridiculous to jail you, the law gets into serious difficulty. It has run out of options.

Time and again the council won pyrrhic victories against the tree campaigners. They would arrest the protestors, cut down the tree and public opinion would turn against them. The more the council hit out, the more draconian they were, the more fire it gave to the protestors' actions. In the end, the protestors made sure that so much time and money was spent on felling each tree that it was just becoming unworkable.

To really challenge the law, you need three things. First you need people on your side. Second, you must be peaceful. Third, your action must be clear; there needs to be a direct moral nexus between your action and what you hope to achieve. In Sheffield, this moral nexus was as direct as it could be. We don't believe you should cut down these trees, so we stand around them to stop you doing it. That's a pretty clear statement.

The Sheffield tree campaign was the most stunning win, and the proudest moment of my life. It caused me and a friend to set up Lawyers for Nature, an organisation that gives free legal advice to people who are campaigning to protect nature. When you're working in the legal sphere, you find out pretty quickly that the law is deeply inadequate to protect nature. First, much of the damage against nature is already illegal, but the laws are not enforced. Second, the law is constantly fighting these rear-guard actions to stop destruction that has already occurred. We need to put forward positive ideas of how we want our relationship with nature to be.

So in 2021, together with about a hundred locals, we declared the Rights of the River Cam. These rights treat the river as a legal entity, giving it the rights of a human. This reading out of the river's rights is completely unsupported by law. But whether it has an effect, whether it actually causes any change, stands or falls on the extent to which people are willing to work towards peacefully upholding those rights. Any law is contingent on someone's willingness to uphold it.

Everyone can go out there, right now, and become a defender of your local river's rights, and if you are prepared to break the law of trespass that stops you, you can change that law and protect your river. Imagine people using water-testing kits all over the country or reporting sewage overspills. If enough people are willing to do that, I believe there could be a huge change in this country. With law, the power doesn't just rest with parliament to create it, or fancy lawyers to interpret it. There is a third way: activism. If we believe that nature has rights, and if enough of us act in accordance with that, it becomes true. It's a kind of magic.

CASE STUDY: WEEKLEY HALL WOOD

Just a week or two before lockdown, planning-permission signs went up around ten acres of local woodland and wildflower meadow in Kettering, Northamptonshire, informing the public that the woods were about to be cut down to make way for five commercial warehouses, a general industry building, service yards, parking, drainage, landscaping, two substations and a pumping station.

Despite being recently confined to their homes, local residents organised a petition, which has, at the time of writing, close to twenty thousand signatures attached to it. The residents lodged over six hundred complaints with the local council, set up a website, wrote a song, created a calendar and did everything they could to resist the passive acceptance of the fate of Weekley Hall Wood.

The application was submitted by Buccleuch Properties, the business end of a large local landowner, the Duke of Buccleuch and the Buccleuch Estate. A spokesperson for Buccleuch Properties said, 'We are very mindful of the value and importance of the natural environment within our local communities, and we believe the application strikes an appropriate balance between what would be a significant economic and job creation boost for Kettering and the well-being of local ecological assets.' Of course, as the landowner, Buccleuch Properties gets to decide the definition of 'appropriate', and the 19,300 locals who signed the petition have no rights whatsoever to save the wood.

Undeterred, the locals attracted widespread support from a wide group of people and local organisations, including the local Labour Party, the Co-operative Party, Greenpeace, Friends of the Earth, the Woodland Trust and many other local organisations. They established themselves through a formal constitution as a community group. They carried out surveys in the summer, which showed that at the weekend over a thousand people used the woods for recreation, and during the week over seven hundred people visited on a daily basis. They read a huge amount of documentation, attended and spoke at many council meetings to try to get councillors to reconsider the application, and they set the modern enclosure in its local, historic context.

In the words of John Padwick, a local teacher, campaigner, parish councillor and historian:

> **There is a historic parallel. In June 1607, four years after James I came to the throne and just two years after the Gunpowder Plot, with its local links with the Tresham family, forty to fifty people (according to letters of the gentry) had been killed nearby by local landowners, including the precursors of the Duke of Buccleuch, the Montagu family, and the Treshams, protesting in a dispute over land rights and the enclosure of common land. The Newton Rebellion was part of the Midland Revolt, a wider movement against enclosure, which has been seen as the last time the peasants of England rose up against the gentry. The king commanded that the insurrection be put down by force if necessary. One thousand people had gathered at Newton, a tiny hamlet, to pull down the hedges and fill in the ditch with which Thomas Tresham of Newton had enclosed the Brand, a patch of common land on the outskirts of Rockingham Forest, between Geddington and Little Oakley, which had been used by the local peasantry for subsistence farming for 'time out of mind'.**

By setting the current crisis of Weekley Hall Wood in a larger context of historic enclosure, the campaigners have linked a small local matter to a wider landscape of injustice, one that not only denied (and still denies) the public access, but which also destroyed (and still destroys) nature, in the pursuit of private profit.

In the particular case of Weekley Hall Wood, the campaigners have, so far, opted for diplomacy over direct action. Being local, they know the specifics of the case better than anyone else and have decided that continuing to negotiate is the best course of action for now. But with the research put into the campaign, the data on public usage, the history that set this modern enclosure in its context and the 19,300 people in support of conserving it, Weekley Hall Wood serves as a perfect template for a trespass story published on TrespassersCompanion.org. So, here is an *imaginary* trespass of Weekley Hall Wood, to illustrate the kind of trespass story we'd like you to contribute to our website.

Today a group of us trespassed Weekley Hall Wood, a beautiful section of woodland just outside Kettering, Northamptonshire. We trespassed these woods because we love them, and because we have been excluded from these woods due to the planned destruction of ten acres of its trees and wildflower meadows at the hands of its owners.

In 2020, Buccleuch Properties applied for planning permission to cut down ten acres of this woodland to build five commercial warehouses, a general industry building, service yards, parking, drainage, land-scaping, two substations and a pumping station.

But this natural environment is far too valuable to be destroyed. On our walk, we spotted a chequered skipper butterfly, previously extinct in England since 1976, but thankfully reintroduced into nearby Rockingham Forest in 2018. Even the duke's planning application recognises the woods' 'significant ecological value', and yet they aim to tarmac it over.

We noticed a great number of bees in the wildflower meadow. A Friends of the Earth spokesperson, Alan Heath, has said: 'If built, the development will destroy a substantial area of countryside and biodiversity. Bees and other pollinators are particularly in decline due at least partly to a loss of 97 per cent of their habitat over the last sixty to seventy years.'

The Duke of Buccleuch owns 280,000 acres of Britain. Recent research by CPRE has shown Kettering to be one of the most nature-deprived areas in England. During lockdown, a survey we commissioned showed that 700 people used the woods for recreation. We need these woods, not just for a thriving ecology, but for our own mental and physical health.

The Duke of Buccleuch's motto is *Amo*, 'I love.' Well, we trespass today under the motto *Amamus*, 'We love.' We love the woods, we love the flora and fauna that live within them, we want to protect them, and we want our families, and the generations after, to enjoy them as we once used to.

PREPARE YOURSELF FOR THE BACKLASH

With trespass, things can get very heated very quickly. The simmering rage of current English culture, recently never far from the surface, is instantly exposed by the act of trespass. On the land, those that confront you may well patronise you, goad you and threaten you, safe in the knowledge that if you react in kind, the law will support them over almost anything you do or say. After the trespass has been published, many comments on social media will be predictably vitriolic, and follow the same tired format of received opinionating. When the *Argus* published news of the Landscapes of Freedom trespass of 24 July 2021, the comments that followed were exactly of the template that followed the Kinder Trespass and just about every protest since. Here are a few choice examples, with a brief semiotic analysis.

> **'The great unwashed doing their "bit" for
> society by encouraging trespass.'**

Cleanliness is a thoroughly fascinating anthropological study and is raised in almost every objection to protest. The idea that protestors are dirty is more than a response to dreadlocks, unorthodox clothing or the mud of a protest camp. Similar to the tired cliché attached to traveller encampments, 'dirty' really means 'out of place', something that defies the neatness of the order than bans the action. The accusation of being dirty is often paired with the notion of idleness, that protestors have nothing better to do. Again, idleness refers to anything outside what is deemed the right and proper activity for a person, and its roots can be traced to the Tudor period, where it was used as a justification for enclosure.

> **'Another day, another soap-dodger's protest.'**

See above.

> **'I wonder how much rubbish you idiotic
> thoughtless people left on you [sic] stroll.'**

The answer, in this particular case, was none. In fact, the only litter visible on any part of the trespass was the empty plastic shotgun casings left by the pheasant shooting that took place on the council-owned land – in other words, the very activity that legitimised the exclusion of the public who paid for it. But of course, the question is not a question, it is a statement – a kneejerk response to public access that pretends that all trespassers are 'of a kind' and that this kind is bad.

> 'When every one of these protesters first opens up their gardens for any one to walk through, day & night, disturb anything planted, dump litter & let their dogs $hit every where, then I will happily support their cause.'

This is the classic retaliation to arguments for greater public access to nature, and one that necessarily ignores any knowledge of actual right-to-roam legislation across the globe. Of course people's private gardens are protected, *of course* they are. But so strong is the notion of threat that it even ignores its own inherent daftness: that groups across the country would be calling for garden invasions, or that the Scottish government actively legislated for it in 2003.

This kind of blinkered outrage is not just confined to the comments section of the media. Baron Moore of Etchingham, most commonly referred to as Charles Moore, former editor of the *Telegraph* and big burly beast of right-wing punditry, wrote in the April 2021 edition of the *Spectator* that the Right to Roam campaign was inciting hatred against landowners: 'If incited by Mr Hayes to hate the people who own much of the countryside, might visitors not chuck litter all over it with even greater abandon than during Covid?' Of course, the real message of this statement was an incitement to hatred against Right to Roam campaigners, which would be a proportionate

response to his claims, if they were in any way substantive. When they asked for a space to reply, to set the record straight, the campaign was refused anything more than 175 words:

> **I can understand how Charles might feel threatened by such an attack on the narrative of his Olde England, but the truth is, much of the common land of England, once shared by us all, was enclosed by walls funded by colonialism and slavery. We have the receipts to prove it. His suggestion that the English might use their greater access rights to our beautiful countryside to scatter Lucozade bottles in an act of uncivil disobedience against landowners, not only completely misunderstands the systemic causes of litter, but also trivialises the severe effects on our collective mental and physical health of being excluded from nature.**

So wrote the Right to Roam campaign, in 105 words, which were never published. There is not much that can be constructively said in reply to statements that wilfully ignore evidence in the pursuit of sensationalism, but it is imperative that civility and politeness are maintained at all costs. Any mirroring of tone or wrathful sentiment undoes the worth of the initial trespass, because it supports the central notion that sustains any orthodoxy – that any challenge to its system is inherently threatening. To maintain civility is to increase the chances that your point will not be instantly dismissed by the contingents most crucial to instigating change: the middle ground.

The middle ground is the mindset between two radically opposed points of view, and whatever the topic, most of England lives there. Politics is not a central concern to the middle ground, and therefore those that live there do not see political points in polarised binary form, but are open to arguments if they relate in some way to their lived experience. Much of the middle ground will agree that access to nature is important, vital even, but they will be concerned about the potential impact of greater public access. Perhaps the most frustrating aspect of the middle ground is that they will say they agree with your point in principle, but not the way you have raised it. Of course, without something dramatic, the point is inevitably lost in the noise of progress, the conversation of change will never be raised, and things will continue as before. Ask Extinction Rebellion: so great is the adherence to orthodox codes of right and proper conduct that the majority of the public are prepared to watch the world burn rather than step over the line.

THE REAL FIGHT

If you're going to really trespass the lines of division and exclusion, you have to climb the mind wall. The biggest barricade in this debate is that of partisanship – not just the idea that one side can't see eye to eye with the other, but worse, that they shouldn't. As Brexit has shown, as tempting as it is to fall into this mindset, it's too simplistic, it doesn't reflect the complexities of an intersectional society, and it simply doesn't help. To live as if you're free already is to meet people as you find them and not abide by labels that pit one side against the other.

There is an orthodoxy alive in England that causes people to defend the very thing that damages them. Often the most vocal opponents of greater public access are those that stand to gain from it. Through a curious mix of Stockholm syndrome and a 'better the devil you know' mindset, they defend the Duke of Westminster's right to exclusive ownership of 129,300 acres of England, while their children make do with a tiny garden and a few rights of way. They feel threatened, they hurl insults, say things they don't really

mean, and all the while the Duke of Westminster remains quiet.

To enter into this matrix of division, to hurl insults back, is to be the puppet of this orthodoxy. It pits the access campaigner against farmers, fishermen or anyone else who has exclusive access rights to

land. But this division is false and helps none but those who have created it. Paddleboarders and fishermen are kith and kin in their love for rivers, and any aggression between either group is simply reading from someone else's script. The real opposition to greater public access to the green and blue space of England is not the farmer, the landowner nor the aristocrat, but instead something altogether more abstract: public consensus.

Public consensus is the mindset of the middle ground, often directed by powerful media outlets, but it can change, of its own will, surprisingly quickly. Public consensus can sway dramatically due to freak events – usually public tragedies such as the Grenfell Tower fire, charismatic campaigning such as Marcus Rashford's 'Free School Meals' campaign or, most elusive of all, a change in the zeitgeist.

Marcus Rashford is the Paul Revere of football, a figure with widespread influence because of an innate natural charisma, but also because of the work he has put into winning people's hearts. A Marcus Rashford can never be simulated or contrived, and as yet, we don't have one on the Right to Roam campaign. However, we are at the beginning of the fallout from a massive freak event, the global public tragedy of Covid-19, and this has caused an undeniable zeitgeist that has reminded us of our deep connection with nature.

If we can rise above partisanship, actively seek out conversations with those that oppose us, find a common ground, then we can change the public consensus to that of Scotland, Norway or Sweden. As long as we're causing no harm, our presence in nature should not be defined as such.

FARMERS

Agriculture employs about 1 per cent of the UK workforce, about 466,000 people in the UK. Agriculture covers around 71 per cent of our land, and produces around 60 per cent of the food we consume, and for every £1 invested in farming support, the industry gives back £7.40 to the economy. Farming is very important.

Farming is getting older. The average age of the British farm holder is now about sixty, and with low pay, high land prices, and pressure from rising costs and falling value, it is failing to attract a younger workforce. With climate-related weather disasters, unforeseen outbreaks and market fluctuations in the price of fuel and feed, the biggest threat to farming in the UK is stress. One small farmer kills themselves every week in the UK. Farming is very, very hard.

Some farmers report receiving abuse from ramblers trying to cut across their land, some report livestock being worried or killed by dogs, some occasionally report damage to crops. Some say that the last thing they need is greater public access, which will not only increase these instances of harm but also, consequently, increase the stress they experience. The opposite is true.

Greater public access to agricultural land is essential to refocusing the country's attention on the value of farmers. Farmers need to be central to local access forums, community groups that keep the communication alive between those who own the land, those who work the land and those who

love the land. Farmers are the nurses of the earth: they know the land like a surgeon knows a body; they keep alive an old relationship with nature that we all once had. For this, they are more than producers of food, but pillars of society, like doctors, teachers, even priests.

The 'get orf my land' trope, that image of Farmer McGregor chasing Peter Rabbit out of his carrot patch, is deeply embedded in English culture, but it is a useless cliché that casts the farmer as a cartoon villain. A farmer's concern for their crops, livestock and machinery rests halfway between a foreman's concern with their building site and a mother's concern for her children; it should be greatly respected, and should be a central focus of any future public access agreements. With local community groups set in place to safeguard future access land from litter or vandalism, farmers need a guarantee that their work will be unimpeded. It is crucial that this conversation happens as soon as possible, so that farmers feel integral to the change of access laws. Right to Roam are seeking a mutual, reciprocal, friendly relationship with farmers and land workers and it is incumbent on the trespasser to create this new relationship. Our trespasses should take us into the future we are seeking. We should forge a code for the New English Countryside and act in accordance with it.

'We want to be a part of the countryside, and we urgently need to reconnect to nature. And until we can have a conversation about how best to make this happen, we will keep coming back.'

RIGHT TO ROAM

We don't just need a right to roam. We need a complete revolution in our relationship to nature. And a right to roam, if introduced properly, is the way we get there.

All across the English countryside stand humble, often overlooked, local-made sculptures that illustrate the very crux of this debate, and which stand as silent metaphors for its resolution: stiles. The stile is the most beautiful human construct of the English countryside. It straddles the divide between public and private, between poetry and pragmatism. Crucial to the effect of the stile is that it doesn't just offer you the assistance to access the countryside beyond the fence, it also acts as a powerful visual encouragement to do so. Just as a gate with a lock around it wards people off, eventually making them forget about the possibilities beyond it, a stile in a fence is not just a licence and a means to cross it, but it also acts as an incitement to do so. A change in the architecture of the law would not only allow and facilitate greater access to the countryside, but crucially, like a stile built into the legal framework, it would actively encourage people towards nature.

But there is another important aspect to the stile: balance. By offering a safe way over the barbed wire, it facilitates the public's right to access nature. And by keeping the fence in place, it facilitates the farmer's and landowner's right to continue their work without risk to crops, livestock or profit. The stile is a balance of interests. And so is the right to roam.

Any expansion of England's right to roam would first need to be preceded by consultation. But unlike the consultation to the CRoW Act, there must be many more people representing many more communities at the table. In other words, it must take the form of a citizens' assembly. This would not only be a chance for every community in England to have their say, but even more importantly, it could be used as a powerful wave of publicity to engage England in beginning the urgent process of improving our relationship with the outdoors, renewing our contract with nature.

The Right to Roam campaign is not about arguing for a few more spaces for people with ski poles and breathable anoraks to walk through. This is the old ideology that has hemmed in our connection to nature with terms such as 'leisure' and 'recreation'. Instead, and much more powerfully, it is about unlocking a sense of belonging to our land, for everybody, in every community in England, and for the land itself. It's not a silver bullet to solve issues of race and class, but there is no question that it will improve the lives of our marginalised communities. Society is rooted in land, and so issues of land affect every aspect of our lives. What single other change of law could promote mental, physical and spiritual health while also allowing people the opportunity to care for nature? What other legislation could tackle both loneliness and the destruction of ancient woodland? The right to roam is the first step over the line towards a new relationship with nature, which could benefit all aspects of society.

THE COUNTRYSIDE CODE

A point of fact: the Countryside Code was not instigated by the government, the National Farmers' Union (NFU), the Country Land and Business Association (CLA) or any of the other self-proclaimed stewards of our land, but by the Ramblers and Open Spaces Society. While campaigning for greater public access to the countryside, both organisations came up against the same story that we face today: the public cannot be trusted in nature. So in 1943 the Ramblers and the Open Spaces Society formed a joint committee to gather information on public behaviour in nature. Their investigations led them to the same conclusion that Right to Roam put forward today: that the central problem is not an inherent, genetic disrespect for nature born into people who don't inherit land, but simply a lack of education and understanding for the working practice of the countryside. The joint committee wrote a comprehensive memo to the minister of education, in which they set out their proposals for a Countryside Code and their recommendations for a mass publicity campaign.

The government did nothing, presumably because there was a war going on. But in 1949, when the National Parks and Access to the Countryside Bill was going through parliament, the necessity of a code of conduct for the countryside was again raised by Earl de la Warr, the first hereditary peer to join the Labour Party, who moved an amendment to require the government to prepare one. The government turned down this motion on the premise that it would be too complicated and too rigid to impose a code of conduct on the countryside. But both the Ramblers and Open Spaces Society, who knew how essential it was, lobbied hard until the government conceded.

Eventually, in 1951, the code was published for the first time. Both the Ramblers, the Open Spaces Society and forty-five other invested voluntary organisations took responsibility for disseminating the code to the public. Over the years, responsibility for the code moved from the National Parks Commission to the Countryside Commission and the Countryside Agency to Natural England, but its core messages have remained the same. When the CRoW Act was passed in 2000, the Countryside Code extended its scope over another 8 per cent of land, but, as Right to Roam have shown, financial support to promote its message almost entirely disappeared.

The most striking conclusion of this history is that the very existence of a code is the direct result of the campaign for greater public access rights. The consultation work to create the code, the lobbying for it and the dissemination of its message has been work almost entirely enacted by groups that campaign for greater public access to the countryside. When the CLA or NFU refer to the Countryside Code and demand greater education, they are in fact quoting the words of the access campaigners they lobby so hard to stifle.

THE CROW ACT

The Countryside and Rights of Way (CRoW) Act was passed into law on 30 November 2000. It opened up about 8 per cent of English land to a responsible right to roam, meaning we, the public, can ramble across it freely, without fear of trespass. The CRoW Act was a major victory for over a century's worth of campaigning, and it has proven highly successful and highly popular. Yet for most people in England, in terms of their mental and physical health, in terms of social equity, it has been next to useless.

Science has proven not only how urgently we need access to nature for our mental and physical health, but also that, for any registrable results, this access must be regular and sustained. So much of English land currently open to public access (mountain, moorland, heath and downland) is remote from the majority of the public, relegating access to nature as little more than a holiday activity and not the regular immersion that our bodies cry out for. On a societal level, the lockdowns endured by this country have proven to us not only how viscerally we need time in the outdoors, but also, starkly, how access to open spaces is critically unequal, dividing the country along those old fault lines of race and class.

The CRoW Act is woefully inadequate to the needs of the twenty-first century. It needs to be extended so that its freedoms actually apply to the majority of the public. It needs to spread its wings to cover woodland, rivers and green belt, the latter of which would make nature easily accessible to 60 per cent of the population. It needs to take responsibility not just for access routes within the countryside, but also for access routes into the countryside, from urban populations. It needs to take responsibility for the bus routes that councils have been forced to cut, landing a direct blow to those without access to cars, a demographic that includes the impoverished working class and disabled and elderly people.

The CRoW Act must recognise the extra work that needs to be done to make sure that the English countryside is not reserved solely for those who own it and those who can afford to rent access to it. It needs to recognise that for people of colour there are barriers to access other than the barbed wire of private estates. The government should be compelled to listen to groups such as Black Men Walk for Health, Black Girls Hike, Black2Nature and Land in Our Names to find out how best to reach out to people of colour, to promote the notion that the countryside is also theirs to enjoy. With barriers such as race and class, it is no longer acceptable to simply designate areas of space as open access; infrastructure must urgently be created to actively encourage and facilitate this access – otherwise it just won't be used.

The Countryside Code needs a radical kick up the ass. The government must allocate more money to promoting the code, to making it more widely known and to actively teaching it in schools. The public have to learn a few lessons about their responsibility to the countryside and to those for whom the countryside is a place of work, by actually experiencing it. Too much of our understanding of nature is theoretical, and most of the basic premises of the code only make sense through a lived experience. As experiments in Scotland have shown, people respond better to being informed – to being told why, rather than just being told.

The CRoW Act needs to take responsibility for litter. The vast majority of the English public who walk in the woods and swim in the rivers do so because they care deeply about its flora and fauna, as well as appreciating what it does to our bodies, our minds and our souls. The problem with us treading lightly and leaving no trace of our presence is that there is no evidence of us having done so. Litter sticks out like a sore thumb; not littering is impossible to prove.

But it is not fair on landowners and farmers to extend the right to roam over their land without guaranteeing that it won't come with more litter. The CRoW committee needs to look to groups such as Surfers Against Sewage or Trash Free Trails, and use their experience and networks to create a model that rolls out volunteer schemes across the country. Imploring people not to leave litter is less pragmatic than facilitating people to pick it up and opens the door to extending our rights of access across a far wider scope of England. People earn access to the countryside by actively engaging with the health of its ecology.

Rights in parallel with responsibilities. A sense of communal work towards putting the land first. Sustainability, interaction and connectivity. All of these ideas are both radical and nothing new; we had them before we were excluded and we called them *the commons*. Extending the CRoW Act would be a dynamic move towards a country that is healthier, more cohesive and more inclusive, and a community that is far more implicated in the survival of its countryside.

THE PEOPLE'S CHARTER
FOR THE OPEN AIR

The necessary extension of our rights of access to nature must not be an isolated act. It must be introduced within a framework that ensures its efficacy and supports its sustainability. The implications of greater access to nature reach into almost all sectors of society, from education, conservation, healthcare and welfare, and each of these sectors must be expected to contribute to its success. For too long, access to nature has been sidelined as a recreational concern; it is much more than this. Access to nature is an issue of health, class, race, gender, disability and parity in society, and must be approached as such. To resurrect Lewis Silkin's phrase from the late 1940s, a right to roam must be part of a wider People's Charter for the Open Air, a covenant between community and environment that changes the whole dynamic of the countryside, from exclusion to inclusion.

The first barrier to fall will be the false notion that community and environment are separate entities. They are not. So much of our society depends on the health of our environment that it is false to partition them. The welfare of our society is the welfare of our environment, and each supports the other.

The People's Charter for the Open Air will reignite our right of responsibility alongside our right of access – not one before the other, but in one go. They are two sides of the same coin. It follows, therefore, that the extension of our rights to access nature depends first and foremost on the Māori notion of *kaitiakitanga*, the active protection of the environment by locals. Each parish of England must have its own guardian group, a team of locals who have specific responsibility towards the health and welfare of the environment within their territory. The guardian group must be representative of the community, and it will act as a bridge between the local population and the owners and workers of the land. Following the Trash Free Trails model, guardians will be responsible for litter and for any damage incurred by public access, and will offer a guarantee to landowners that a right of public access will not damage their workplace. The New English Countryside will balance the needs of the landowners with the needs of the public.

But the guardians can also offer much more. With their local knowledge of the area, with their direct line of contact between land workers and owners and the public, they can act as a hub for education and action that

benefits the environment. Guardian groups will coordinate with local schools to create education plans that are situated in local nature. They will coordinate with bushcraft schemes, forest-school camps, initiatives that not only teach a fuller knowledge of the outdoor world but also a responsibility to nature and to each other; they will ensure that these essential experiences are open to all children, regardless of economic background (this will be possible because entry to the countryside will be free). Guardian groups will coordinate citizen-science schemes, from monitoring water pollution and invasive species, to a much fuller recording of the health and diversity of our species. Every parish has a local historian, a local botanist, enthusiasts who are willing to share their knowledge and experience for the simple love of sharing. In the New English Countryside, amateurism will be celebrated and supported as a keystone of our connection to nature.

The guardians can go even further. If England needs to double its tree cover, from 10 per cent to 20 per cent, why not use these groups to organise local tree planting, an act that will bind the community to each other and to the forest for generations to come. It will also offer huge savings to the public purse, no longer needing to finance professional organisations to do the same work. During the drought of 2020, largely unreported due to the pandemic, local residents of Oxfordshire were recruited by the Hardwick Estate to water the saplings that had just been planted to balance the loss

of several hundred ash trees from dieback. The young trees were saved from death by the free labour of locals, who were all keen to extend their connection with nature from simply observing it to actively helping it. The forest that grows as a result of their labour will be a manifestation of society and environmental cohesiveness; it will be a living expression of the commons. This tiny example could be extended across England, creating not just one generation of guardians but families of them, so that children can walk in the woods their grandmothers planted. That's how we build a sense of belonging in the New English Countryside.

We can go further still. When Scotland introduced an expansive right to roam in 2003, it also legislated for a community right to buy. The Land Reform Act stipulated that a local body, made up by members of the community, could register their interests in purchasing land, provided that their acquisition was 'compatible with furthering the achievement of sustainable development'. Most recently, in May 2019, locals of Langholm – a burgh in Dumfries and Galloway colloquially known as the 'Muckle Toon' – clubbed together to buy Langholm Moor, owned by the UK's largest property owner, the Duke of Buccleuch. They crowdfunded £3.2 million to buy the property and completed the purchase in October 2020. They now work together to manage 5,200 acres of land, which will become a hub for community interaction, with each other and with nature. Rather like the collective ownership of a pub, practised across English villages, locals have a stake in the management and sustainability of the land and feel more deeply implicated in its future. They all pitch in, graft together and have a deeper connection with the environment and with their community (because they are one and the same thing). The New English Countryside allows communities to manage the land they live on.

English nature is in crisis. Irrefutably, we need to dedicate more land to the thriving of nature: we need to protect it from further destruction and encourage its regeneration. Rewilding makes perfect sense. But look at it again through the prism of land rights, and the rewilding movement is no less exclusionary than the aristocratic system of monopolised stewardship, the archaic, paternalistic, centralised decision-making that excludes everybody else. Under this system, children's education is still excluded from nature; our understanding and emotional connection with the countryside remains severed. Instead of rewilding, the People's Charter for the Open Air will encourage *recommoning* – a flourishing not just of nature, but of the communities' relationship with nature, because the future depends on everyone caring about the environment, not just those that own it.

The responsibility to forge a New English Countryside is on all of us, but the government must not shirk their responsibility. They must consult with a far wider group of stakeholders and create a much more robust countryside code, one that accepts our right to swim, camp and lay fires, and as such, gives urgent practical codes of conduct that have been ignored until now. We should look to the Scottish Outdoor Access Code as a model for our own – not just in its content, but in its format. It must be reviewed every five years, acknowledging the premise that the management of a right to roam is flexible to dialogue, negotiation and changes in context.

The right to roam is an incredible opportunity to save the Treasury much of the £8.2 billion per year it spends on our sedentary lifestyles. So the government must speculate to accumulate. To fund an architecture that makes the English right to roam work for everyone would be to make these savings incremental and sustained, to benefit the nation in the long term as well as the short. The New English Outdoor Access Code should be properly funded. But its entire communication strategy must also be redesigned. Why shouldn't the code be upgraded to suit the twenty-first century, and speak to new generations in a manner they feel comfortable with? The New English Outdoor Access Code should be an ongoing social media campaign, complete with celebrity endorsements. It will communicate to us in a manner suitable for the modern age.

A right to roam would of course invalidate almost every sign currently excluding the public across the English countryside. We have options. We could remove the tacky signage and dispose of them as the single-use plastic waste that they are. The more solid signs, the metal and hand-painted wooden ones, could remain and become the focus of walking and paddleboard tours, to remind people of the value of what we have gained. Alternatively, we could do away with signs altogether, and, god forbid, have a place on earth that is not designated, branded and codified with human interest. Let the New English Countryside be a place where we go not to tell or be told, but to learn, watch and observe, to experience the workings of nature, the passing of time, the changing of seasons. But if we do decide on signage, let them be new, neat QR codes, placed at points of high visitor volume. Instead of telling people simply to go away, these signs will take you to a centralised website, updated seasonally by the guardian groups, informing you of how the land is being used, your responsibilities to each particular site and what to look out for. The New English Countryside welcomes you and wants you to learn about it.

It would then be the government's responsibility to offer landowner grants for the installation of suitable architecture to facilitate use – in other words, stiles. But it is their role to consider infrastructure as well: bus routes should be reinstated from urban populations into areas of nature, and these renewed routes should be publicised with great fanfare. But why not point people to the countryside from areas of dense urbanisation? Why not put up signs in the centre of Birmingham, for example, that point people out to the countryside, to the nearest green space, to Warley Woods, or the bluebells in Coldlands Woods, both within eight miles of the city centre? The New English Countryside both facilitates and encourages people towards it.

Of course, we need to decide exactly what an English right to roam would actually look like. Our English rights must be compatible with our English countryside. Should we follow the Scottish model and encourage wild camping, mountain biking, wild swimming, paddleboarding and so on, across all but specific areas of the land, or should we focus on extending the CRoW Act over areas such as woodland, rivers and green belt? What is certain is that alongside a right to access more of the countryside, we need a right to do more than just walk. For people's physical and mental health, we need to be able to exercise in a way that we enjoy, because that is the key to sustained exercise. Why should a swimmer be

made to walk, when swimming is what they love?

For too long we have accepted the piecemeal advancement of rights, a bargaining table of bartered compromise that treats our connection to nature as squares on a monopoly board. The backstage negotiations of the CRoW Act must be brought forward into the limelight and must take the form of a citizens' assembly. Alongside the Country Land and Business Association, the Countryside Alliance and the National Farmers' Union, English rambling, canoeing, mountaineering and cycling must all be represented. We must be honest about the barriers of race, gender, class and sexual orientation that block people from nature, and we must tackle them directly by centering representatives from those communities at the heart of discussions. Whoever we are, wherever we live, wherever we are from, we are all shareholders in nature. Commoners need seats at the table.

Chris Sharp

Right to Roam's Citizen Assembly manager

Our democracy isn't working. This isn't a contentious statement. It's something most of us, even in our polarised and divided political communities, would agree with. I'll briefly outline the problem with our current democratic system and then suggest a solution.

Governance is the process of making decisions. And good governance is about making the right decisions. But time after time, our leaders flagrantly make the wrong ones. This isn't entirely their fault: their job is absurd. In the UK, ministers change roles constantly; one day someone is the transport minister, the next they're chancellor of the exchequer. This means they need to understand the intricacies of an integrated national transport network one day and the full scope of the nation's economic affairs the next. What other job would expect you to have such a diverse range of expertise? But it doesn't really matter because our system of government is modelled on the monarchy, which means it funnels all the real decision-making power to the person at the top.

But the job of the person at the top is even more impossible. With the buck stopping with them, they have to be experts on literally everything. It doesn't matter if we reform our system to select 'better' leaders. The world is just too complicated. It wasn't always. At the dawn of the scientific revolution, when many of the ideas for our democratic system were being devised, it was possible for a single person to know everything there was to know. Now even the most exceptional person can't be expected to have the sheer quantity of knowledge required to make decisions on the vast array of controversies and emergencies. Our leaders have advisers and experts to guide them, but even with help they have to listen to information on an enormous variety of issues – vaccination policy, artificial intelligence, the viability of marine cloud brightening, the wisdom of international trade deals and the mental health benefits of a right to roam – absorb all the complexities and competing interests, mull it all over and then decide what action to take. We should not be surprised that this system is not producing good results.

Churchill famously said 'democracy is the worst form of government, except for all those others that have been tried'. This is often quoted, but it doesn't really make sense. Which type of democracy was he referring to? There are many different flavours. Our current system is a delegative democracy, where we vote for others to do our governing for us. The House of Commons is supposed to be a venue for discussion and debate. But the reality is some six hundred people grunting, shouting and jeering at each other in a manner that sounds like they're trying to mimic the belches of the seventeenth-century landed gentry. The UK has also dabbled with direct democracy through referendums, and we have a vast network of think-tanks, lobbyists, social media, private interests and media barons contributing to the democratic decision-making process and taking power from the people. Our delegative democracy is leaving us feeling powerless, voiceless and that our votes don't count.

The solution is a new form of democracy. Or, actually, an adaptation of an old form. The form Aristotle would have recognised. That of Athens, democracy's birthplace. A system of democracy structured around deliberation, negotiation and dialogue.

This form of democracy attempts to emulate some of the features of the creation of scientific knowledge. Science, practically speaking, is the most successful system ever devised for getting to the right answer. How science works is complicated and still hotly debated, but basically, science is a social enterprise. The idea of the lone genius sat in a lab creating new knowledge is a myth. Scientific knowledge is socially constructed through interactions between informed groups and individuals communicating, reviewing, debating and cross-pollinating ideas through dialogue. Science is dialogic. Our decision-making processes should be too. We should create a dialogic democracy. One way to do this is through citizens' assemblies, which use the template of science to come to rational, informed answers to controversial and complex societal questions. The way it works is simple. A citizens' assembly or jury – there are many designs, but they all work in essentially the same way – is selected from among the population through the research technique of representative sampling. The participants are then taught the facts and ethical debates of the issue. This process of education is essential to making informed decisions. Experts provide the information but do not contribute to the negotiations. Their role is simply to inform. Once educated, the participants discuss the issue. They engage in dialogue, raise concerns, listen to arguments and assess responses. It is this process of deliberation that deepens understanding and helps the group to coalesce around a decision. Then they vote on the matter.

The governance decisions made by citizens assemblies, in areas as diverse as solar geoengineering and nanotechnology, have been good, displaying understanding and appreciation of political, social and ethical nuance. They have even been surprisingly radical. The BBC documentary *The People vs. Climate Change* held an experimental assembly where members of the public attended a three-month process where they were educated on the science and ethics of climate change and left to talk with each other, in the canteen, socially, online and in organised meetings. The process generated proposals including a tax on frequent flyers, a ban on fossil fuel home heating and measures to reduce meat and dairy consumption by 40 per cent.

These proposals were given to an MP, who raised them in the House of Commons, where they were roundly ignored. But perhaps our leaders should think of the opportunities dialogic democracy presents. Sitting alongside delegative democracy, maybe our leaders would appreciate deferring some of the difficult decision-making to the people in a way that differs from a referendum because of the education element. But the thing is, to make real change, the decisions of a citizens' assembly need to have actual power – the weight of law. If participants believe their decisions will be enacted, they will act in a manner that reflects the responsibility they have, understanding their direct impact on society. We don't feel a sense of responsibility in our delegative democracy. Our system encourages divide and rule. A dialogic democracy has the potential to solve controversial problems, and to bring together powerful and engaged citizens.

AN OPEN LETTER

... to *Landowners*

We trespass your land not in defiance of you, as the law currently defines it, but to express our love of nature, and our desire to be more deeply connected to it. We trespass your land in order to start a conversation.

Like other countries across Europe, including Scotland, Estonia, Norway and Sweden, we believe that a connection with nature is a birthright, not a crime. But with the English public forbidden from 92 per cent of the land and 97 per cent of rivers, the scale of our exclusion is neither justifiable nor tenable. Something must change.

In 2016, the 'State of Nature' report pooled data from over fifty conservation and research organisations and found that the UK was one of the most nature-depleted countries in the world. But, without a connection to nature, it is no surprise that many people find it hard to comprehend the scale of our climate crisis and habitat loss. As the scientist Robert Michael Pyle wrote, 'What is the extinction of a condor to a child that has never known the wren?' People need a connection to nature in order to care.

Our health is declining, our NHS is cracking under the pressure. Physically, we are suffering through our sedentary lifestyles, with both heart disease and obesity on the rise; mentally, we are faced with urgent crises of stress and depression. Science has shown that all of the above are linked to nature-deficit disorder, and that the symptoms can be alleviated by a renewed connection with nature. We trespass because we know, in body, mind and soul, that nature can heal us.

The coronavirus pandemic has revealed the extent to which exclusion from nature is an issue of class and race, of justice as much as fairness. As research by the Office for National Statistics, the Campaign to Protect Rural England (CPRE) and others have shown, it is the poorest and most marginalised communities that are the least likely to own any green space of their own, the least likely to live in a nature-abundant area, to live in proximity to a national park or area of outstanding natural beauty (AONB) or to have the transport available to enjoy them. Wherever we live, whatever our income, whoever we are, the right to access nature should belong to us all.

The Countryside and Rights of Way (CRoW) Act allows us to wander freely on 8 per cent of the land. But since much of this open-access land is remote to much of the population, its benefits have been profoundly limited. To see a registrable effect on our nation's health, we need to access nature regularly, which means we need it near to our homes. When rivers can regulate our stress levels, when woodlands can fortify our immune systems, when the open space of green-belt land can offer us room to exercise, why are we forbidden from so much of our landscape? We need to bring CRoW to our doorsteps.

We appreciate the concern that access to the land has not always been met with respect for it. But when so many of us grow up excluded from nature, when the government has been spending just £2,000 a year on publicising the Countryside Code, is it any wonder some people don't know how to behave responsibly? When the Scottish Land Reform Act of 2003 and the CRoW Act of 2000 opened up the land to the public, they also placed clear definitions on our responsibilities to it. Rather than inviting negligence into the countryside, extending our rights of access would allow the nation to forge a new relationship with the land, to learn and educate ourselves about the proper way to respect the countryside and its workings. Ignorance is the real threat to the countryside. A full right to roam would reboot our connection to nature, and teach us first-hand the responsibilities we owe it.

We appreciate that the countryside is a place of work. But we also see that your work is undervalued by society. Rather than interfering with your work, greater access rights would allow us a better recognition of the essential labour you put towards our lives and our society. We envision a future in which people come to the countryside not just to be in it, but to support and improve it in partnership with those who live and work within it. For our environment to survive, for our society to thrive, our countryside cannot simply be the preserve of those fortunate enough to own it. We want to be a part of the countryside, and we urgently need to reconnect to nature. And until we can have a conversation about how best to make this happen, we will keep coming back.

Yours respectfully,
Right to Roam

... *to the Ramblers*

We have the greatest respect for what you have achieved over the last eighty-odd years. Your work in advance of the 1949 National Parks and Access to the Countryside Act gave the nation national parks, national trails, the definitive map of rights of way and national nature reserves. With the CRoW Act, you secured a right to roam over 8 per cent of our land, and you have been fundamental to the development and future completion of the England Coastal Path. Your volunteers maintain our rights of way, and many are helping to preserve more footpaths from being lost for ever.

But let's be honest, 8 per cent of access land in England is bugger all, and whatever happened during the CRoW negotiations to make swimming an act of trespass on open-access land is sheer absurdism. That needs undoing; and because you were integral to the CRoW negotiations, you share that responsibility. Your goal, as expressed in your mission statement, is 'to create a Britain where everyone has the freedom to enjoy the outdoors'. But in England especially, the stark truth is that very few of us enjoy this freedom. If you really want to make England a nation that benefits from the experience of nature, then you need to address the largest barrier: our exclusion from the countryside by law of trespass.

Your current position on extending our rights of access to nature is that 'now is not the time'. But, frankly, this is a position of privilege. If you step outside the perspective of the largely white, able-bodied and financially secure demographic of your membership, you will see there are so many communities in England whose lack of access to nature is in urgent crisis. One that needs sorting right now.

You have over 100,000 members, all of whom love the countryside with a deep passion. To galvanise these members into supporting the campaign for a right to roam would undoubtedly help to swing the debate. We know that you play a delicate role in bridging access rights for the public with the orthodoxy of the landowning establishment; but we both know that many of your members, staff and board support a greater connection to nature. So now, more than ever, for the health of the nation, it is the time to show leadership: *support the right to roam.*

Yours hopefully,
Right to Roam

... to NHS Workers

First and foremost, thank you. You have guided our nation through a tremendous crisis, and we have felt safe in your arms. You have worked tirelessly, without adequate support, and we cannot begin to imagine the toll this has had on your bodies, your minds, your personal lives and your emotional well-being. We applauded you from the rooftops, even though many of us had started to feel like it was a little more than a jingoistic charade: the insistence on calling you heroes in a transparent attempt to divert our attention from the real issues at hand, the empty rhetoric when all you needed was supplies. But still we clapped, because it was the only way to show you that we are, from our heart, all of us, so very deeply grateful. Only the government can offer you the wages you deserve. But perhaps we can offer something else: time. At righttoroam.org.uk, we are working towards an England that is more connected to nature, and healthier for it. By allowing you to focus on treating our ailments, rather than maintaining our health, you will have more space in your hospitals and surgeries, and more time to administer the world-class care you offer. You will be happier in your work, more capable of administering your expertise. On top of all this, your budget won't be so relentlessly drained by the impact of our sedentary lifestyles, which will allow you to experiment and test to further our knowledge of care; to practise science.

Like you, we have read the peer-reviewed papers; like you, we know how nature can improve our mental and physical health. We want to act on this science. For too long has access to the countryside been seen purely in terms of leisure and recreation. But it is worth much more to us. Nature is the missing link in healthcare; access to nature is access to well-being. We would love your support as we make these points to the government. Sign up to our campaign at righttoroam.org.uk and come join us on our peaceful and joyful trespasses.

With limitless gratitude,
Right to Roam

A DETAILED
INVESTIGATION
INTO THE
MORAL
JUSTIFICATION
FOR THE
EXCLUSIVE
OWNERSHIP
OF LAND

In the absence of any moral justification for the exclusion of the general public from nature, please use this space for notes.

Make no mistake, there is a real land movement in England. Separately, these organisations, large and small, have been growing in influence and scope over the last decade, and only recently are they beginning to interact with each other and support each other's work. This is more than solidarity; this is momentum.

Check out these websites and see for yourself the network of people and organisations working to make nature and humans more deeply entwined, and to make that connection more sustainable and reciprocal. A much more detailed map of the interconnected land movement can be found at landjustice.uk.

TrespassersCompanion.org

The companion of this companion: download posters and memes, upload your trespasses and research modern enclosures.

righttoroam.org.uk

The mothership: sign up here to become part of the movement for an English right to roam. Watch videos, download resources and learn more about the argument for greater public access.

whoownsengland.org

Who owns our country matters. It matters because land is a scarce resource – as Mark Twain put it, 'They aren't making it any more' – and because ownership of it often confers wealth, power and influence. It matters because who owns land gets to choose how it's used, and that has big implications for almost everything. Where we build our homes, how we grow our food, how we protect ourselves from flooding, how much space we set aside for wildlife – all this is hugely affected by who owns land.

geographypaul.com

If you happen to be an educator, you'll find a superb teaching course here set up by award-winning teacher Paul Turner. Being a radical geographer, Paul has created a course that incorporates the sociology, history, politics, economics, religion and biology of land rights, and is a primer course like no other. Like another radical, Henry George, he holds up a prism to society that demonstrates how fundamental access to land is to every element of our society.

The Land Is Ours
tlio.org.uk

The Land Is Ours campaigns
peacefully for access to the land
and its resources and the decision-
making processes affecting them,
for everyone, irrespective of age,
race or gender. Their website is a
phenomenal resource of historic
and current land rights issues.

House of Annetta
houseofannetta.org

House of Annetta is a new centre
for land reform and spatial justice,
systemic concerns that are both
produced by and in turn reproduce
our economic order. Created by
Assemble, the Turner Prize-winning
architecture and design collective,
House of Annetta is a new home for

criticality of the current land system
and an environment in which to
nurture alternatives. If you're in
London, they're located at 25 Princelet
Street, just off Brick Lane. Everyone is
welcome to pop in and explore.

Three Acres and a Cow
threeacresandacow.co.uk

Three Acres and a Cow is a stage
show that connects the Norman
Conquest and Peasants' Revolt
with climate change and the
housing crisis via the enclosures,
the English Civil War and the
Industrial Revolution, drawing
a compelling narrative through
the people's history of England in
folk song, story and poem. Check
out their wiki page, a Creative
Commons performers' kit for the

English show. Each module has an overview of key points and themes to be communicated, some sample text and a list of songs, poems and stories that could be used to illustrate them.

Land In Our Names (LION)
landinournames.
community

LION is a grassroots, Black-led collective committed to reparations in Britain by connecting land and climate justice with racial justice. LION aims to disrupt oppressive land dynamics relating to people of colour in Britain. They address land justice as a centre point for issues of food insecurity, health inequalities, environmental injustice and widespread disconnection from nature.

Black2Nature
facebook.com/OfficialB2N

Black2Nature's objectives are to work towards the increase in engagement of visible minority ethnic (VME) people with nature and the environment, through education, to understand the benefits to physical and mental health and well-being and how that can relate back to their rural heritage abroad.

Black Girls Hike
bghuk.com

Founded in 2019, Black Girls Hike provides a safe space for black women to explore the outdoors. Challenging the status quo, and encouraging black women to reconnect with nature, they host nationwide group hikes, outdoor activity days and training events.

Black Land and Spatial Justice Fund
uk.gofundme.com/f/black-land-justice

This fund has been developed to redistribute resources, including finance and knowledge, engaging in decolonial frameworks and collective organising to redefine our relationships to land and space.

Nature Is a Human Right
natureisahumanright.earth

An organisation that is on a mission to make contact with nature a recognised human right. To build towards this goal, they are raising awareness of the issues at hand through campaigning, partnerships and publications, as well as petitioning for legislation and policy change at a local level, and supporting grassroots action.

Lawyers for Nature
lawyersfornature.com

Lawyers for Nature were set up to give legal assistance to all those who campaign to defend nature from destruction. From the Sheffield tree campaign to Stop HS2 and Extinction Rebellion, they offer pro bono legal advice to keep our nature defenders out of prison. In their own words: 'Currently, the lawyers working for large companies and developers, seeking to develop and build on green space, vastly outnumber the lawyers advising those groups seeking to defend their local environments. We seek to redress this legal and power imbalance, through the use of our volunteer network, knowledge database and in-development legal advice clinic.'

But they are also going one step further. They are at the forefront of the campaign to give nature the legal rights of personhood (in other words, its own rights), so that individuals or companies that poison and destroy our rivers and trees can be brought to justice.

Shared Assets
sharedassets.org.uk

Shared Assets CIC is a 'think-and-do tank' that believes that by changing our relationship with land, and by working together, we can build a future that is fair, equitable and just. They undertake consultancy, research and movement-building work to support, mobilise and advocate for the development of models of managing land that create shared social, economic and environmental benefits.

Land Workers' Alliance
landworkersalliance.org.uk

LWA is a union of farmers, growers, foresters and other land-based workers with a mission to improve the livelihoods of their members and create a better food and land-use system for everyone. They work for a future where producers can work with dignity to earn a decent living and where everyone can access local, healthy, affordable food, fuel and fibre – a food and land use system based on agroecology and food sovereignty that furthers social and environmental justice.

Resisting Anti-Trespass
ra-t.org

RA-T is a decentralised network of squatters and vagabonds resisting the enforcement of the new anti-trespass measures included in the upcoming police powers: the unauthorised encampment bill, first announced in the 2019 Tory manifesto. To fight this bill, which endangers our very ways of life, they are calling for autonomous actions. They support a diversity of tactics.

People's Land Policy
peopleslandpolicy.home. blog

The People's Land Policy is a project to develop discussion and debate about what kind of land reform we need. By bringing together a range of people to discuss land and the issues that affect them, they are contributing to the building of a broad-based radical movement for land reform.

The Land Magazine
thelandmagazine.org.uk

The Land magazine is the mother tree of the land movement. It is written by and for people who believe that the roots of justice, freedom, social security and democracy lie not so much in access to money, or even to the ballot box, as in access to the land and its resources.